Silent Hill 2

Silent Hill 2

Mike Drucker

Boss Fight Books
Los Angeles, CA
bossfightbooks.com

ISBN 13: 978-1-940535-27-2
First Printing: 2020

Series Editor: Gabe Durham
Associate Editor: Michael P. Williams
Book Design by Cory Schmitz
Page Design by Christopher Moyer

For everyone at Dillard High School who told me
Silent Hill was scary but "not that scary"
and then it was very scary.

CONTENTS

WHAT IS
SILENT HILL 2?

Writing a book about any "classic" video game always carries the threat of nostalgia poisoning. Does a specific gameplay cycle work because it evokes fun or because it only evokes memories of fun? Do vintage graphics hold up because of their artful design or because the writer had them on their bedsheets twenty years ago? That is to say, it can be easy to confuse an appreciation of art with an appreciation *of an appreciation* of art.

Fortunately, *Silent Hill 2* is not a nostalgic game.

Sure, I remember playing Konami's survival horror masterpiece for the first time in high school. I even remember the game blowing my dumb high school mind. I wouldn't be writing this book if I didn't. But unlike *Super Mario Bros.* or *Street Fighter II* or [insert your favorite retro game], playing *Silent Hill 2* today resists that feeling of comforting fondness because it is neither comforting nor fond.

Before we go any further, if you haven't played *Silent Hill 2*, go do it now. Unfortunately, unless rumors of a remake become true, that's easier said than done. Too bad; it's worth it. Buy a PS2 or Xbox online and hunt down a used copy. The game was also released on PC, but until an online store like GOG puts it up for sale digitally, tracking down that CD-ROM is quite a task too—let alone applying fan-made patches to make it work on modern operating systems. There's even a *Silent Hill 2* "Enhanced Edition" unofficial upgrade to the game. If you absolutely have to, the Xbox 360 version of *Silent Hill HD Collection* works on modern Xbox systems, even though it butchers the experience by switching up voice actors and losing atmospheric graphical effects.

Did you put down the book and play the game? Of course you didn't, so here's a quick refresher.

At its core, *Silent Hill 2* is a 2001 survival horror game in the vein of the early entries in Capcom's Resident Evil series—a third-person action adventure in which the player moves from area to area, blasting through enemies and solving puzzles.

Progression through the game is relatively linear; you might get turned around in an apartment building and miss an item here or there, but there remains a relatively straightforward path Konami's designers expect you to take. Area maps—as well as their helpful automatic markings when you find blocked or locked doors—make it almost too easy to find where you're supposed to go next. For all the series's narrative themes of mental confusion and isolation, you as a player rarely get "lost" in *Silent Hill 2*.

Combat also follows standard late 1990s/early 2000s survival horror: You can run or fend off baddies with weapons such as wooden planks, guns, or (if you know how to get it) a giant knife. As was, and still is, often the case in the genre, ammo and healing kits are always in short supply. Occasionally, you'll come across "bosses"—hulking monstrosities that serve more as dramatic bullet sponges than they do actual in-game threats. This is especially true of the ever-popular "Pyramid Head," a recurring enemy with—you won't believe this—a pyramid for a head. Meanwhile, combat difficulty is adjustable at the start of each run, making the game both more accessible to fans and easier on writers who have to play this gauntlet of sadness over and over again to try to get every ending.

Between all the running and fighting are small puzzles that require logic, items, and paying attention to your environment. These puzzles range from the bizarre to the deeply disturbing—from an in-game trivia challenge to figuring out which of six hanged corpses in the Labyrinth was innocent of a crime. Completing these puzzles rewards you with further game progression or much-needed items. Hints and riddle-like solutions are usually available nearby, and, like combat, the puzzles' difficulty can be adjusted before starting the game.

But gameplay isn't the main reason *Silent Hill 2* is so fondly remembered. It's the tale of James Sunderland and his late wife, Mary, that makes the game truly special. Our protagonist receives a letter from the long-dead Mary asking him to return to their "special place," i.e., the town of Silent Hill. As James moves through various locations, such as rotting apartment buildings and a moldering hotel, he learns the truth about his marriage. Spoiler alert: The truth about his marriage is that he murdered his wife. So that's fun.

While James is the only playable character in the game, he's far from the only one lying to themself—and us—about their past.

The seductive Maria just happens to look identical to Mary (and is played by the same amazing actress, Monica Taylor Horgan). Both a romantic interest and foil, Maria alternately flirts with James and taunts him, an echo of his toxic marriage. Maria also repeatedly dies in cutscenes throughout the game, only to later appear alive as if nothing happened at all. Yet the player ultimately has more control over her fate than the game lets on: In-game actions can determine outcomes such as Maria leaving town with James or becoming the final boss monster.

Then there's Angela, a suicidal woman who was physically and sexually abused by her family. We first come across Angela in a mental fog, searching for her mother in a graveyard. Later, we learn that Angela murdered her father and possibly her brother—adding guilt to the intense shame of her abuse. Her story ends with her ascending a flaming staircase into—well, we don't know what! Let's talk about it later!

Meanwhile, Eddie is an awkward man-child who spent his life being bullied for his weight. This once led to Eddie allegedly lashing out by severely injuring a tormentor and killing their dog. Throughout the game, Eddie's paranoia and rage only grow: He eventually accuses James of bullying him and becomes the only boss battle against a regular human being in the game. Unlike Angela or James, Eddie relishes his rage, unconvincingly bragging about his body count to impress others around him.

Young orphan Laura, however, seems wholly unaffected by the town. She skips and laughs through locations filled with monsters, spending less energy on escaping than she does taunting James. Yet Laura's anger seems to be justified. Mary was set to adopt her before she was murdered by James, which itself hides an even greater mystery: If Mary died years ago, as James believes, how is Laura the same age? Spooky. Not as spooky as a tragic murder, granted, but still.

Some of these questions are left entirely up to the player's imagination. Others are somewhat clarified by the game's multiple endings, which themselves are again realized through mostly minor, seemingly inconsequential decisions made by the player. It's very possible for those delving into the game without a guide to find themselves at an ending and have no idea how they got there—or think it's the only one.

But that's not to say that gameplay is just window dressing until the end. As critic Ewan Kirkland puts it in his paper, "Restless Dreams and Shattered Memories": "Silent Hill is a town populated with traumatised protagonists struggling to deal with repressed memories, often externalised in the form of monsters and boss creatures which must be battled in order to complete the game." Forcing players to confront trauma through gameplay makes *Silent Hill 2* a deeply unpleasant experience.

It also makes the game one of the first mainstream titles to seriously deal with trauma, bullying, depression, abuse, and suicide. And it's still one of the best; *Silent Hill 2* remains as compelling an experience today as it did nearly twenty years ago. The game exists on its own terms. Its characters and monsters and themes beg for continued play and critical consumption—hence the book you're now reading.

While obviously not the first game to tell a story, *Silent Hill 2* was a primordial prototype of the two decades of narrative-driven exploration games that followed. Playing it never feels nostalgic, and outside of the game's slightly dated controls, it never comes off as a "throwback." If anything, the game feels *more* at home today than it did in 2001.

Whereas critics at the time expected big action and hard jump scares in their survival horror, many games today—especially indie horror games—have taken cues from the slow build and discomforting sense of loss in the Silent Hill series and especially *Silent Hill 2*. Even beyond straightforward survival horror, echoes of *Silent Hill 2*'s slow breakdown of complicated relationships can be seen in games such as *Layers of Fear* (2016), themselves more exploratory horror titles.

Silent Hill 2 remains a vital experience because it respects itself and its audience. The game isn't long— yet it tells an emotionally complicated story within just a handful of hours. We're never overfed exposition on characters—there's no "evil plan" to reveal, no dossier to pick up that explains everything.

Less is more here, and *Silent Hill 2* nails that mantra at every step. The fog, woefully removed in the HD remake, hides enough of the town to keep it feeling both vast and claustrophobic. The voice acting perfectly hints at each character's place in their own psychological nightmare—Eddie's anger, James's denial, Angela's trauma. The light music, industrial sounds, and the intermittent radio static that warns of nearby danger all paint a world that somehow both exists outside of us as players and entirely in James's head. Even what we hear shows instead of tells.

It can be insulting to a game to say "the story is all that matters," but *Silent Hill 2 drives* its story *through* the gameplay. The more we play, the more hesitant we are to continue playing. Without the ability to get bigger or stronger, each step is more worrisome than the last. With each discovery that James isn't what he appears, we're less compelled to want to help him. The game makes us question ourselves and our role in a cycle of violence.

Silent Hill 2 remains popular because its self-contained ambiguity gives us space to think, to imagine, to discuss. We play again and again to learn more about what happened to Angela and confront Eddie's response to bullying. We want to figure out just *what* Maria is, or why Laura is safe from monsters. We relive the game, just as James relives his punishment over and over again—each time trying to unlock the experience a little more. The fact that *Silent Hill 2* only tells you *just enough* to move forward is what makes it worth returning to every time.

So turn on your radio, grab a crowbar, and take a trip with me through the worst little town in America.

Also, play the game. For real.

THE SURVIVAL HORROR
BANDWAGON

SILENT HILL WOULDN'T EXIST without *Resident Evil* (1996). Not because it was great, but because it was successful. Capcom's horror classic inspired many companies to look at its interesting story, terrifying monsters, and survival-based gameplay and think: "We could make some money off of that!"

True, *Resident Evil* didn't invent scary games; 1992's *Alone in the Dark* featured many of the same horror elements we now associate with the genre. And *Resident Evil* itself is a spiritual successor to Capcom's own *Sweet Home* (1989) on the Famicom. But *Resident Evil* did coin the term "survival horror" in 1996, and it was the first successful console title to pull together disparate elements to create a far grander experience.

Resident Evil may feel slow and plodding now, but it's a damn jet engine compared to *Alone in the Dark*. *Resident Evil* has puzzles like those in horror games such as *The 7th Guest* (1993) and *Phantasmagoria* (1995), but doesn't focus the entire experience around being a master of unlocking. The game's graphics don't quite hold up, but at the time they captured a cinematic B-movie quality that would make George Romero proud. In fact, George Romero even wrote a script for the *Resident Evil* movie, although it was eventually rejected.

The immediate success of the newborn franchise led to sequels, merchandise, novelizations, and movies. Almost overnight, *Resident Evil* became a multimedia empire. It also led other companies to flood the market with their own survival horror titles. As *Silent Hill* director Keiichiro Toyama explained in an interview with the *Official U.S. PlayStation Magazine*, the original inspiration for his game was less David Lynch and more Merrill Lynch: "The original concept actually came from the corporate side; they said we should try our hand at making a horror game."

But while Toyama and his team tried their hand at horror, another team at Konami was readying the next entry in their biggest spooky franchise: Castlevania. Castlevania games were packed with zombies and vampires and werewolves—seemingly the perfect fit for the burgeoning 3D horror craze. So Konami released *Castlevania* (1999), an atrocious Nintendo 64 game plagued by poor controls, level design, and pacing. With one foot in the past and another foot in the future, the old guard of scary games suddenly lost its scary.

Silent Hill, on the other hand, was a brilliant sub-version of the Resident Evil formula before that formula was even stale. *Resident Evil* and *Resident Evil 2* both featured elite police officers blasting away massive monsters with increasingly large and more explosion-y weapons. *Silent Hill* swung the pendulum the other way. As Ewan Kirkland explains in his article "Masculinity in Video Games": "The Silent Hill series is notable in this respect: a commercial franchise that works within generic and industrial constraints, yet manages to challenge traditional models of masculinity and their implication in conventions of video-game characterization, representation, and play." There are no battle-hardened super police in Silent Hill, just regular people having a really bad day.

Playing a regular Joe blew my mind as a teenager. The hero of the first game, Harry Mason, got tired. He was weak. He was a scared dad on the run, not a super soldier. His fear translated to my fear. As a bullied, tired kid, I immediately connected with the exhausted, sad character on the screen.

So did critics. *Famitsu* gave the first game a 34/40. IGN scored it a 9.0, calling the game a "much more cerebral approach to the horror genre." Meanwhile, GameSpot gave *Silent Hill* an 8.2, saying it "establishes a very unsettling atmosphere that at once puts you off and creeps you out," although they did criticize the game's story as lacking a solid "payoff." Audiences nevertheless paid Konami plenty, with the game going on to sell 1.6 million copies.

Naturally, Konami believed that the game's fascinating, unique world could be the jumping off point for more wonderful art. And by art, I mean money. Development soon started on *Silent Hill 2*. Once again, Konami subverted expectations. Whereas Capcom had made *Resident Evil 2* a bigger, badder, extension of the first game, Konami kept the creepy town of Silent Hill and basically threw out everything else.

For a wonderful, brief period of time, Silent Hill appeared to be an anthology series like *Black Mirror* or *The Twilight Zone*. Characters would change. Stories would change. In an interview with IGN, *Silent Hill 2* producer Akihiro Imamura said, "The stories [in the series] aren't really linked. *Silent Hill 2* is the story of another man that takes place in the town called Silent Hill. Basically the setting itself that is the town of Silent Hill is the same. But it's a different area of the town."

Imamura later goes on to draw a rough map of the city, marking the different areas where *Silent Hill 1* and *2* take place. This drawing isn't canon; it's a metaphor for the differences between the feel of the two games. It's like saying, "*This* part of Silent Hill is evil because of a cult, while *this* part represents the purgatory of a man who murdered his wife." Judging from this interview, Imamura and Konami appear slightly anxious about the audience's response to *Silent Hill 2* not being a real sequel. True, *Silent Hill 2* includes minor references and symbols to the cult from the original game, and later entries in the series retconned a much stronger connection. But at the time, Inamura wanted the game's audience to know the new game's experience would be different than they might expect.

Of course, unrelated game sequels were common by the time *Silent Hill 2* was released. Outside of a few spin-offs, the Final Fantasy games' stories rarely connect in any meaningful way. The Legend of Zelda games also barely overlap, confusing multi-dimensional timelines notwithstanding. This is true: I worked at Nintendo for a couple years, and I *still* don't understand the Zelda timeline.

The first two Silent Hill games get the best of both worlds by centering the *setting*. As Kirkland puts it, "There are suggestions that the town of Silent Hill represents a beacon to particularly troubled individuals, for whom the landscape and the creatures within it assume a reflection of their own inner turmoil." The town connected the first two games, not their stories.

At least for a while.

It's bittersweet to imagine a future in which the Silent Hill series stuck with this innovative path. Almost all of the series's sequels and prequels, including *Silent Hill 3*, do their best to tie themselves to the narrative of the original game. Some of the games even do it well!

Silent Hill 3 is a pretty great survival horror game! But in my opinion, it lacks the heaviness and sorrow that define the first two games. You can find me online for your hate mail regarding this opinion.

Only 2009's *Silent Hill: Shattered Memories* comes close to the level of experimentation found in *Silent Hill 1* and *2*. A re-imagining of the first game, *Shattered Memories* refocuses the story on psychology and player panic, replacing all combat in the game with powerless fleeing. It's a strange, highly enjoyable take on the series that sold a fraction of what the first game did, which is a real shame.

Meanwhile, if you went by all the merchandise and cheap spin-offs, you could say that the basic blueprint of the series is that it takes place in Silent Hill and there are undead nurses with boobs. Besides the eight games in the main series, there's been a Silent Hill light-gun game, a Diablo clone, and a pachinko machine—all of which are more interested in the game's gruesome monster design than in atmosphere or story. But original game director Keiichiro Toyama detailed a narrower approach to the series in a 1999 interview with *PlayStation Magazine*.

> It will be easy to outline Silent Hill's characteristics if we look into the two main concepts that we focused on from the start. One is that the game was supposed have a "modern American novel" type of

atmosphere. A traditional town in the countryside is the setting for the game, where it creates the weirdness and the eeriness in the ordinary world. […] [W]hat the team was most inspired by were the cult movies from the 70s and the 80s and maybe the Science Fiction movies from the 50s, more than the modern horror novels, actually. There are some cult icons that appear in the game, but those were just some added points to build a frightening feeling.

It's important to remember that Silent Hill is a game series designed by a Japanese team but largely inspired by American art. As Silent Hill series composer and producer Akira Yamaoka put it, "The original *Silent Hill* was our attempt at making classic American horror through a Japanese filter." *Silent Hill 2* producer Akihiro Imamura especially noted the work of David Lynch and, in particular, his television show *Twin Peaks*. Like *Twin Peaks*, the Silent Hill games take place in a small, isolated town in which everything seems one step removed from the "normal." Character designer and series co-creator Takayoshi Sato also cites David Lynch as an influence, along with Alfred Hitchcock, David Fincher, and David Cronenberg, all of whom have work in which the normal is twisted to feel unnatural.

Sato also mentions the 1990 horror film *Jacob's Ladder* as an inspiration, and that makes sense: The two share a lot of similarities. The movie follows a Vietnam War veteran whose sanity comes into question when he begins hallucinating terrifying monsters around him. Some of these monsters would fit right in with a Silent Hill game, such as a doctor whose eyes are entirely covered by skin. Even the setting of the movie would be familiar. While it takes place in New York, the main character occasionally finds himself trapped in what appears to be a nightmare world. One scene follows him being rolled down the hallway of a rotting, rust-covered hospital filled with deformed people. It's a clear inspiration for the rotting, rust-covered "Other World" that characters in the Silent Hill games experience. Even the ending of *Jacob's Ladder* matches one of the endings from both *Silent Hill* and *Silent Hill 2*, although we'll get to that a bit later in the book.

Sato has also cited the Irish painter Francis Bacon as an influence, and it's not hard to see why. Take, for example, the 1944 painting, *Three Studies for Figures at the Base of a Crucifixion*. Three gray, shapeless figures with disturbingly human mouths appear to scream and suffer against a backdrop of bright red. Each figure in the painting could easily take the place of monsters such as *Silent Hill 2*'s bed-meets-flesh Abstract Daddy. Not for nothing, those paintings make *great* desktop backgrounds when you grow up as a goth kid.

Bacon's other paintings, such as *Study after Velázquez's Portrait of Pope Innocent X*, featuring what appears to be a religious leader screaming as he disintegrates, are just as good a fit for Silent Hill. They evoke a timeless punishment, which is very much the point. As Bacon himself said, "I would like my picture to look as if a human being had passed between them, like a snail leaves its trail of the human presence… as a snail leaves its slime."

Twin Peaks, Jacob's Ladder, and the work of Francis Bacon all succeed at making the mundane uncomfortable. They manifest underlying cultural anxieties as something physical. Games critic Kevin F. Steinmetz refers to this as a "breach" of prison imagery into the mundane in his article, "Carceral Horror: Punishment and Control in *Silent Hill*": "Prison imagery thus appears to abjectly infiltrate and disrupt the game environments, frequently appearing in otherwise 'unreasonable places, as if to remind the player that they—via the in-game avatar—are ensnared."

Silent Hill started as a commercial project intended to capitalize on *Resident Evil*, but where it went next was somewhere far more interesting. Rejecting the lavish mansions and gothic mood of other popular horror games, Konami's new series focused on something far more terrifying: the secrets and fears in our everyday lives.

A PECULIAR
LITTLE TOWN

AT FIRST GLANCE, Silent Hill is the type of town that high school students can't wait to leave. It might be a nice place to visit, but at its best, the most "fun" location in *Silent Hill 2* is a bowling alley. Sure, there's also a strip club, but it appears to be about 40 square feet with a bar containing maybe one bottle of booze. I'm not a great judge of strip clubs, but I am from Florida, which brings its own qualifications. I'm pretty sure you need a little more space than you'd get in the average studio apartment.

Yet from the very start of *Silent Hill 2*, we're forced to confront the disconnect between the banal and the abnormal horrors just underneath the town's surface.

The "town with a secret" is a common trope in both Eastern and Western horror. Take, for example, the town of Kurouzu in Junji Ito's amazing 1998 graphic novel *Uzumaki*. Everything seems normal in Kurouzu until people become obsessed with spirals. This quickly—wait for it—spirals into violence and destruction that the characters can't escape, no matter how hard they resist. And like Silent Hill, the curse is permanent—there's no "fix" or "unfinished business" the characters can solve to make things right. What happens in Kurouzu stays in Kurouzu.

Twin Peaks, again a direct inspiration for the town of Silent Hill, is filled with the contrast between an exaggerated Americana-inflected goodness and an equally exaggerated weird horror beneath the surface. While *Twin Peaks* is never quite "normal," you have all the small-town America tropes of an episode of *The Andy Griffith Show*—the friendly waitress at a diner, the light-hearted sheriff who just wants to do right, the bad boy, the beauty queen. But they're all subverted and twisted by their own dark secrets.

One quote from the show's Sheriff Harry S. Truman could've come from any character in Silent Hill and fit perfectly within literally any one of the games:

> *Twin Peaks* is different, a long way from the world. You've noticed that. That's exactly the way we like it. But there's a... back end to that that's kind of different, too. Maybe that's the price we pay for all the good things. There's a sort of evil out there. […] Call it what you want—a darkness, a presence. It takes many forms... but it's been out there for as long as anyone can remember.

In fact, an item in *Silent Hill 2* called "The Book of Lost Memories," discoverable only after beating the game, has a passage about the history of the town that feels similar:

> The name comes from the legend of the people whose land was stolen from them. [...] According to legend, this was where the holiest ceremonies took place. [...] In those days, this town went by another name. But that name is now hopelessly lost in the veils of time. All we know is that there was another name, and that for some reason the town was once abandoned by its residents.

At the center of every town with a dark secret is the dark secret itself. This often comes in the form of a confrontation with colonialism, the cliché of building a town on an "Indian burial ground." In fact, *Silent Hill 2* implies a conflict with an indigenous population that lived there before the city had a name. Some locations in the game are themselves built over previous atrocities, such as the case of the Silent Hill Historical Society existing on top of a Civil War–era prison. There are fewer *un*-haunted places in Silent Hill than haunted places in Silent Hill. Even the bowling alley where we meet Eddie feels wrong and corrupted.

This theme also pops up over and over in the towns of H. P. Lovecraft stories. In "The Shadow over Innsmouth" (1931), a man investigating an old seaside town finds ruined buildings and strange residents who, of course, end up belonging to a cult that made a pact with ancient beings in exchange for wealth and survival.

The story's cult, the Esoteric Order of Dagon, is a prototype for decades of horror novel, movie, and game cults such as "The Order" in the first *Silent Hill*. And much like James in *Silent Hill 2*, the narrator in "The Shadow Over Innsmouth" realizes he was drawn to the town of Innsmouth for a specific and pretty sad reason out of his control. Here, the protagonist turns out to be one of the dreaded fish people who make up the cult and inhabit the town. The narrator's fate was sealed before he even entered Innsmouth. Or put another way, you don't just show up to a town with a secret by mistake.

Stephen King himself refers to these cursed areas as "The Peculiar Little Town", which sounds more like the first song of a light-hearted musical than it does a description of places such as Derry, Maine, where the titular "It" rises every 27 years to feed on fear, haunt dreams, and generally be a downright rascal. Once again, we have a seemingly normal town where the people are influenced and morphed by an ancient evil at the center of the town's history, with people who leave the town being compelled by some supernatural force to return.

Therein lies the tension between the comfort of suburbia and the horror we fear exists underneath. The prison imagery of Silent Hill—bars, grates, and poor living conditions—undercuts the comfort of a sublime lake town, just like it does in real life. For all the comforts and conveniences of modern American life, we still have one of the highest incarceration rates in the world. Right next to comfortable homes and modern conveniences are prisons filled with hundreds of people forced to work for almost no money, many of whom are locked up for non-violent offenses. Konami got their American town more American than they ever knew.

The presence of these spaces also emphasizes James's inability to escape his guilt—or his wife's revenge, depending on both your reading of the story and the ending you get. Silent Hill is supposed to be James and Mary's "special place," a home to beautiful buildings and beloved memories. So what does it mean that James returns to a rotting, abandoned town? Probably that things aren't great.

In the opening of *Silent Hill 2*, we find James in a rest stop bathroom, looking at himself in the mirror. It's a mundane setting, and James is a mundane white dude. Which brings up another point: *Silent Hill 2* is very white. I would say all white. Yes, the game is developed by a Japanese team. But, whether intentional or not, that

Japanese team's idea of an average All-American town with a dark past is suburban and pale.

Artist and designer Takayoshi Sato's characters emphasize this "average" white suburbia (albeit with designs sometimes based on real-life celebrities). James could be anyone. The other characters we meet aren't surprising. None of them would stick out in a crowd. They're coded as *belonging* in this boring town—and getting drawn back to it when they leave. And much like the town itself, each of these average-looking (white) characters have a dark secret.

Design choices like this ground us from the start. That bathroom we begin the game in could be anywhere. Even the filth and graffiti on the walls seem... normal. This isn't a surprising space, but it is one that is unpleasant. Scholars Inger Ekman and Petri Lankoski refer to this as a "contaminating" element. A dirty bathroom is normal, yet its very filthiness acts as a gateway to the rest of the town's rot. It's cool. You get it.

The European release of *Silent Hill 2* included a bonus documentary, *The Making of Silent Hill 2*. In it, designer Masashi Tsuboyama explains one reason for designing Silent Hill to be an isolated town instead of something more "urban" and modern like Raccoon City:

> At the beginning of the game we deliberately made the descent through the forest towards the cemetery longer. It's so long

you don't feel like turning back. At the same time, it makes you realize just how totally isolated the city is… We knew it was a bit risky in terms of gameplay, but we really wanted to take our chances and do it.

Let's talk about the last point first: Sacrificing gameplay for the sake of the atmosphere. During the opening of *Silent Hill 2*, you do… well, nothing. The "survival" part of "survival horror" doesn't start until later in the game than you'd expect. In contrast, *Silent Hill* introduces the action of the game by having a monster burst through a window minutes after your character wakes up in a diner. It's a clear play on the famous dog-jumps-through-the-window scene of *Resident Evil*, an attempt to establish action-based stakes for your character.

Silent Hill 2, however, takes its time. To Tsuboyama, creating a sense of place within the town of Silent Hill was far more important than emphasizing the dangers inherent in it. Not to mention that walking a long path through fog until you find yourself in a graveyard is a *pretty* strong symbol for death. In *Silent Hill*, the opening cinematic finds Harry driving with his daughter, crashing his car, and then waking up to find her missing. But in *Silent Hill 2*, we see James's car already parked. He drove here alone, and there's no accident to kick off the action. James isn't captured by the town like Harry—he's walking into it by choice.

This uncanny isolation drives the horror of the game. Silent Hill is abandoned. It's wrong. And the things you fight in Silent Hill often feel as trapped as you do. The city is run-down, looking as if nature ran its course and reclaimed the town. Homes are abandoned. Cars are rusted. The remains of what look like industrial accidents block off highways. Businesses are closed forever. The feeling is less, "You have nowhere to hide," and more, "Where is everyone and what the hell am I supposed to do now?"

The apartment buildings in particular make conventional spaces uncomfortable. The repetitive layouts and furniture of apartment after apartment creates just as much confinement and anxiety as Pyramid Head. Even in the best of times, it's hard to imagine Silent Hill's Wood Side or Blue Creek Apartments as a place where anyone was excited to be. They're the types of buildings a sitcom dad would live in after a bad divorce.

Part and parcel with this sense of isolation is a desire to learn *why* we're so isolated. Here, bodies and debris leave mysterious clues as to what happened. There's no exposition, just our best guess from the material we can find. Much of *Silent Hill 2* is closer to locales such as the empty house of *Gone Home* or the abandoned vaults of the *Fallout* series. In its own way, *Silent Hill 2* is an early form of the "walking simulator"—a game whose story and experience relies more on exploration than it does direct character action.

Silent Hill's setting is so effective because it pulls back the curtain on "modern." As we all learned during the coronavirus epidemic, even the most familiar places can become prisons of isolation. We may not hear air raid sirens and monster-hinting radio static, but we can become trapped in our homes and neighborhoods, caught following familiar patterns day after day as the world around us falls apart.

Although the game is largely a pastiche of dark Americana, *Silent Hill 2* did copy some locations from the real world—such as Derwentwater Lake in England, and the Church of San Pedro in Ávila, Spain. And comically, some architecture, furniture, and signage in *Silent Hill* was directly stolen from horror movie classic *Kindergarten Cop*. Setting a horror game level in a school identical to one in a cute 90s comedy is just another way to invert the "normality" of the small town setting.

In fact, *Silent Hill* succeeds in its world-building so well that many fans have misidentified a *real-life* location as the inspiration for the city. Centralia, Pennsylvania is an abandoned town with an underground coal fire that's been burning for decades. Buildings remain empty as streets crack and toxic smoke literally pours from the Earth. For years, the rumor was that Silent Hill was largely based on both the story and look of Centralia. I even used to spread the rumor myself because *it looked so true*.

One clue Silent Hill wasn't based on the *abandoned* town of Centralia, Pennsylvania is the fact that Silent Hill isn't exactly *abandoned*. There's nobody around, and that's, you know, really, really creepy. But the implication is that everyone just vanished—or that the town is rotting before your eyes. Televisions are turned on. Lights flicker. Cars are parked.

Complicating this further, the Silent Hill *movie* based on the games is *itself* based on Centralia. What do you do when there's a famous American town rumored to be the inspiration for a famous Japanese video game? Use it! The Silent Hill of the movies was moved to West Virginia, another coal-heavy state. And unlike the games, the Silent Hill of the film series is a ghost town filled with ash instead of fog.

Centralia may be mostly abandoned outside of a few illegal squatters, but it certainly isn't forgotten. It *was* a community of people once, even if that community was forced by the government to relocate. There's a casual ease at which we forget that lives were uprooted and ruined by the disaster. Chernobyl is now the setting of a television drama and science fiction games—horrifying tragedies quickly become entertainment for later generations.

According to Duncan Fyfe's article "Survival Horror" in the *Campo Santo Quarterly Review*:

Centralians themselves couldn't be less happy about *Silent Hill*, since the brief association the film made between Silent Hill and Centralia is now one of the better-known things about the town. Like, what if everyone knew the name of your hometown, but only because Frank Booth in *Blue Velvet* mentioned that he once went to the toilet there.

Inevitably, those who visit Centralia for its relevance to Silent Hill leave disappointed. Every article that posits the town as "the real Silent Hill"—or as "The Actual Town from Hell", "Hell on Earth", "A Ghost Town... On Fire", or as one of the "10 Scariest Places on Earth"—includes a comment section with at least one reality check. "It is NOT a scary place at all." "I'm afraid if you want scary, find an abandoned insane asylum, because Centralia is not very scary at all." "It's very peaceful actually."

There's the rub. There is no real Silent Hill. And if there were, what would you expect to be there? Empty houses? Eldritch infrastructure? Broken streets? Folks, you can find that in *most* of America. So why are we so compelled to lock Silent Hill onto a familiar place or memory? To quote games journalist Leigh Alexander, "American fans of *Silent Hill 2*, for example, are always trying to disassemble it: Is the world of *Silent Hill* this actual 'split' place, a real world, a fog purgatory, and then a hell world? […] That's what Americans do to *Silent Hill*. They want it to be literal."

Fans want the town to be a real place because it already feels so personal. The town looks like it can be visited and, even more importantly, returned to. Silent Hill is a familiar proximity of a town with familiar-ish stores and people who fit into specific hometown archetypes. The cop. The nurse. The husband. The bullied kid. What would our lives be if one more thing went wrong—if the place that we felt most safe also was the place we hurt someone we loved?

Like James, we want to visit Silent Hill. We want to know what's in the fog—if there's punishment or absolution or simply home.

YOUR VILLAIN, JAMES SUNDERLAND

JAMES SUNDERLAND IS BORING.

Seriously, those of you that played the game—describe the physical appearance of James Sunderland to me right now. If the first thing you went to is "generic white guy," congratulations. With his plain face, plain hair, and flat demeanor, James is so generic that he could smother his wife with a pillow and never get caught. You know, like he actually did.

Video games are full of "strong" male archetypes: *God of War*'s hypermasculine Kratos, *Metal Gear Solid*'s gruff Solid Snake, *The Last of Us*'s grizzled and distant Joel. They're the fantasy of being stronger and more powerful. And because the characters are fantasy, we feel comfortable with their preternatural ability for violence. It makes more sense that Master Chief can survive an endless horde of aliens running towards him. It makes less sense that I, Mike, a large adult boy-child, would survive in the same scenario.

Yet *Silent Hill 2* doesn't revel in power fantasies, it reverses them. James Sunderland is a brilliant character because he, well, lacks character. While he may not be a muscled soldier, he's the sort of generic straight white male protagonist that video games have asked us to identify with for decades. When the game subverts those tropes, it's a surprise.

As Kirkland writes in "Masculinity in Video Games," "if spatial progression within video games satisfies traditionally male fascinations with expansion and conquest, Silent Hill repeatedly frustrates such pleasures." It is, after all, an actual horror game and not an action game with horror elements. If James were a grizzled space marine like the Doom series's Doomguy, we wouldn't feel as afraid of Pyramid Head. It's a little less nerve-racking to open the door to a creepy hotel building if you've got body armor and a plasma cannon. You can't have a power fantasy if you lack power.

There's an intentional flatness to James, even in his personality (voiced by Guy Cihi). James reveals very few details about himself and his personal life—most of which come in pieces throughout the game and relate to his marriage. We don't know what James did for a job, what he likes and dislikes, or even how he feels about his life. Outside of his mission to find Mary, James seems to barely exist.

If you had taken a long road trip after receiving a letter from your dead wife and you made a pit stop in a bathroom, and said bathroom was filled with rust and feces, would you really spend that much time looking in a mirror? It's as if the player is supposed to feel more horror than James himself.

James is so singularly focused that we immediately wonder if something is wrong with him. At the very least, he's so disconnected from the utter strangeness of the town that he ironically fits right in. James shouldn't belong in Silent Hill, but he does. In fact, corpses scattered throughout some areas in *Silent Hill 2* use the same design as James; he's literally part of the landscape of the town.

As soon as James leaves the bathroom (our only gameplay option up to that point), the game jumps to another cutscene outside said bathroom, a wide shot showing James's car parked askew, door still open. It's worth noting the role this cutscene plays in distancing the player from James. As games scholar Andrei Nae writes in the article "Immersion at the Intersection of Technology, Subjectivity and Culture: An Analysis of Silent Hill 2," "In *Silent Hill 2*, we see James Sunderland from a third person perspective, sometimes from an angle in which we, as humans, could never position ourselves." In other words, at times we appear to be literally seeing James from the town's perspective, not his.

This is also the first time we receive in-game information about why James came to Silent Hill in the form of a letter from his late wife Mary that is read aloud for the player. Yet it's information James already had—he came to Silent Hill because of the letter. We're only hearing about it after his decision is made. The choice to come to Silent Hill isn't ours to make. It's the first hint that we may be controlling James, but we don't really know him.

At the start of the game, there's no indication James killed his wife. We don't even know much about his wife other than the fact that she died and sent him a letter. The opening feels sympathetic to James—we're led to believe that *he* really believes he could find his wife. As far as we know, he's a mourning widower, not a murderer. While it's easy to fill in those blanks in retrospect, it should be remembered that the original *Silent Hill* featured a generic protagonist similar to James who was searching for a child he *didn't* murder beforehand.

So right away, James is unreliable and arguably imbalanced. He says that "Mary died of the damn disease three years ago. So then why am I looking for her?" Oh James, James, James, you know Mary didn't die from a disease! You killed her yourself, you sappy, depressed murderer! Replaying the game now brings out two strong possibilities: James has had a complete dissociative break; or he's in denial—and we, as the observers of his actions, are part of the denial. The player is present, the player has agency over James, yet the player cannot understand James.

This is the fun of *Silent Hill 2*'s psychological horror. Whereas Harry immediately knew he wanted to save his daughter in *Silent Hill*, it's less clear what James's ultimate goal is. Does he want to save Mary or finish the job? He's certainly curious as to why his formerly-alive spouse sent him a note, but everything from James's parking to his voice hints at confusion and fear. He's in a figurative and literal fog.

While I'm not prone to use secondary materials, such as game guides, the American manual for *Silent Hill 2: Restless Dreams* (an expanded version of the game that includes the "Born from a Wish" extra scenario) indicates that James fears he may be the victim of a hoax. I don't know if this was the developers' intention, but we can at least infer from James's slow, melancholic character introduction that he won't be an action star running into town to blast away the baddies and throw his wife over his shoulder. If he's facing a hoax, he's confronting it slowly.

Gameplay at this point is simple running and exploration. A short walk down the street, James finds a fenced-off wall that reads "Welcome!" in giant letters. Whereas the gates of Hell in Dante's *Inferno* famously read, "Abandon Hope All Ye Who Enter Here," the gates of Silent Hill's Hell celebrate James's arrival, as if the horrors inside were made for him.

Soon we meet our first gross flesh monster. While walking down yet another creepy street, James telegraphs an upcoming encounter with comments such as, "Are these marks... blood?" and, seeing a monster walk into the distance, "That shadow just now..."

We're also introduced to the series's famous radio static. As *Silent Hill* and *Silent Hill 2* relied on fog to help ease graphical processing, monsters were relatively hard to see. Static—ostensibly coming from a little radio James picks up—alerts the player to a nearby foe, even if they can't see them. When I first played *Silent Hill*, the static scared the shit out of me far more than the monsters did; what I couldn't see was scarier than what I could.

Which is ironic, because even as we finally meet monsters, James keeps the same basic muted emotional range he has at the start of the game. James's reactions to the horrors of Silent Hill should be, well, horror. Instead, he's flat, as if himself in fog. Or what he's seeing isn't completely unexpected.

In fact, we routinely find James hinting that he knows more than he's letting on, long before we discover he murdered his wife. Usually the cutscenes go something like this: James confronts a situation or character. The character hints at James having a darker past than he's admitting. James ultimately ends the conversation mentioning Mary and letting the sentence trail off at the end. James is petulant and avoidant—yet simultaneously is trying to be a "hero" in his search for Mary.

TechRaptor writer Roberto Grosso attributes much of this to James suffering from PTSD:

> The PTSD that James suffers from is never really mentioned directly in the game but heavily implied. The guilt of his wife's death, coupled with his involvement in her assisted suicide, has disturbed James heavily. [...] It is through this the true horror of *Silent Hill 2* manifests; it can happen to any of us. Those feelings of despair, loss, grief or anger are all emotions we control at all times, but lose control when the hinges are replaced.

James is a man who's always at the edge of understanding, always in denial, and always afraid to step over the line and admit to what he did. Just as Grosso and I disagree on whether or not Mary's death was an "assisted suicide" (it feels murder-y to me), James himself seems unsure of the intentions behind both his quest and his actions. As players, we don't have much control over moment to moment story choices, limiting ourselves to dive deeper into James's trauma as we dive deeper into the horrors of the town.

The longer James spends in Silent Hill, the worse it gets and the more we learn about him. At one point, we find ourselves in the Silent Hill Historical Society, a museum seemingly dedicated to teaching visitors how much that town sucks. We're forced to explore down beneath this museum into increasingly decrepit rooms and halls, learning more about the town's terrible past as we go. The same applies to James. The further we get into this adventure, the less we like what we find.

James's interactions with Laura, the orphan, put this problem into focus. Laura is a child who taunts James throughout the game, often sprinkling in hints that she knows James hurt his wife. James becomes increasingly anxious around Laura. Even as he attempts to "save" Laura by chasing her around town, she becomes the conduit of his rage. In the hospital, James screams "Liar!" at her when Laura says she had seen Mary recently.

James's anger here isn't righteous, it's pathetic: He's shouting at an eight-year-old girl. It's also out of the players' control—as if James's emotional outburst was outside his own. While fighting monsters and exploring buildings for clues, the player has complete control. As soon as those clues turn into a narrative cutscene, we lose that control and James again becomes confused and erratic.

Here, it's again important to distinguish James from a regular antihero like Kratos. In 2018's *God of War*, Kratos is portrayed as a self-rehabilitating god-killer. He's completely capable of tearing apart divine beings with the chains attached to his arms—but he'd *much rather* be a parent. Antiheroes may be dangerous, but they're safely couched in familiar heroic "might makes right" tropes.

James is the inverse. He hides a dark secret beneath layers of weakness and normality. It's fitting that he looks like he'd appear as a suspect in an episode of *Dateline*, a show famous for its "he seemed like such a nice guy" true crime stories. James doesn't hold back his power, he hides his past. He's not trying to be redeemed; he's trying to deny.

We need this mystery, this driving force in the story. *Silent Hill 2* doesn't have a conventional villain. Sure, it's got unpleasant characters and monsters—and even memorable big baddies like Pyramid Head. But none of the enemies actually seem to have any clear internal needs apart from wanting to kill James.

This is what makes James such a perfect villain for the game. James is just like Silent Hill: unassuming, a little boring, and entirely rotting from the inside. The further James goes, the worse Silent Hill becomes, and the more those around him suffer. Like James, we as players see it through for selfish reasons—the dopamine rush of completing a game or solving a mystery to "find out what happened." We know it won't end well, but we don't care.

As we drive James's narrative, we as players give him the space to act out his shame and guilt and anger. By playing out his violence, and that violence being acted out on manifestations of his own guilt, James pushes himself further and further into his own personal Hell. In hiding information from us—whether intentional or not—James makes us complicit in his actions.

James isn't an antihero.

He's the villain.

HOW DO YOU SOLVE A
PROBLEM LIKE MARIA?

LET'S START OFF BY DRIVING this boat right onto the rocks: Maria was designed and written by men to be physically appealing to men in a game where her function is to follow and seduce a man.

You could even argue that with her sexy voice and her early 2000s Christina Aguilera–inspired outfit, Maria represents the old guard of video game damsels in distress. Do you have to protect her while she follows you? Why, yes you do. Does she drive a moral choice for the male main character? Why, yes, she does. Is she often playful and sexy in a tone-deaf way? Oh, absolutely.

But whereas Maria seems to play the role of an attractive, sexually appealing prize for James (and the player) to earn, she undercuts it by also being an exact physical copy of the wife he killed. We're trained by escort missions to see Maria as a damsel in distress, but it's very possible to end the game with her as a final boss.

Yet Maria isn't a femme fatale, either. She may be cartoonishly seductive, but she never seems intent on consciously betraying James. At times, Maria seems lost in her own story, as if she herself doesn't quite understand why she's in Silent Hill or how she came to be. And whether or not she becomes a final boss relies entirely on the player's actions, even if they're not aware of it. She, in other words, seems to lack the agency to even decide if she's good or bad. It's up to us.

But then there's the *Silent Hill 2* side chapter, "Born from a Wish." "Born from a Wish" was only included with later releases of the game. If you played *Silent Hill 2* in September of 2001, you were out of luck. The short prequel to the main story stars Maria waking up in the town of Silent Hill and searching for a reason to live. You know, super cheerful stuff. "Born from a Wish" complicates Maria's arc further by making her less of a ghost or reflection of Mary and turning her into her own fully-formed character controlled by the player as she faces some of the same monsters seen by James.

It's like having Greedo shoot first—if Greedo got an entire tragic backstory and was an attractive woman. Sorry, Rodian fans, Greedo can't "get it."

Despite the use of the term for certain re-releases of *Silent Hill 2*, it's not a "Director's Cut" of a movie where the new scenes are woven in. Nor is it an extra chapter or an "expansion" that you unlock after finishing the original title. Instead, copies of the game that feature "Born from a Wish" allow you to choose whether to play that first or the main game (now titled, "A Letter from Silent Heaven").

The easy answer for newcomers is to first play "A Letter from Silent Heaven," if only because it's listed first in the menu and marked as the main scenario and "Born from a Wish" is listed second as the "sub scenario." If you play Maria's story first, you find out right away that James killed his wife. Which, you know, spoils the (*waves hands at entire story*) surprise.

"Born from a Wish" also assumes you already understand the mechanics of the game. There's no scaling up the difficulty as there is in the main game, or space to "learn the controls." Players quickly find a weapon and monsters. The chapter isn't hard, but it definitely throws you right into the pool without any floaties.

So let's start from the main game and work our way back to Maria's chapter. James first encounters Maria at Rosewater Park, a place that he had believed he might expect to find his late wife. The scene is strange, almost dreamlike. James explains that Maria looks like she could be Mary's twin, while Maria teases James for his confusion. There's a push-and-pull to the conversation—the more Maria flirts, the more confused James appears to be. Mid-conversation, he even forgets his wife is dead, which is a little weird.

Throughout the game, Maria dominates conversations and has a self-awareness that James lacks. Maria is confident, sexy, funny. She stuns James—after their first conversation, he literally walks the wrong way. James seems more affected by meeting Maria than he is meeting an enemy made of a straitjacket of flesh.

Obviously, we the players know that Maria is, well, *something* supernatural. If a duck looks like your dead wife and quacks like your dead wife, and is a duck in the same town that your dead wife loved… you get the point. James somehow doesn't see this. After his shock wears off, he accepts the reality of Maria at face value. There's a tension between the player controlling James and the character of James himself. It's like being in a movie theater and shouting, "Don't go in there!", except it's our job to make him go in there.

This is all further complicated when James and Maria themselves end up looking for Laura together: James's mission to find Mary is subsumed into helping Mary's doppelganger and the child Mary intended to adopt. If Maria's aggression and sexuality is a stand-in for what Mary could've been to James, Laura is a stand-in for their future—the child they never had.

Yet for all the rescuing, neither Laura nor Maria seem to need saving! Laura hops and skips through town without any danger, while Maria picks and chooses her moments of vulnerability. After evading more monsters, we come to the bowling alley and Maria… doesn't want to come in? After pleading with James to protect her, she'd rather wait outside! You know, outside, where it's totally safe from all the monsters you just spent half an hour blasting to get to the bowling alley.

Maria is helpless… until she isn't. She's kind to James… until she isn't. The game forces the player to protect her and then throws it back in their face. It all emphasizes how easily James—and, by extension, we—are manipulated.

James and Maria soon move on to the strip club Heaven's Night—with the implication that Maria works there when she pulls a key out of her boot and afterward oddly seems to return it to both her boot and her bra. Okay, well, there's technically no actual in-game model for the key, so it's hard to tell what exactly is happening. But you get the idea. Even Maria's literal job is to be an object of desire.

In the documentary *The Making of Silent Hill 2*, Sato says that Maria's motion-captured facial expressions weren't to his liking, so he did them by hand. In a metaphorical and literal sense, Maria is handcrafted to be compelling.

Maria is using James's sexuality to confuse him. Although a less generous interpretation is that the game's designers couldn't resist moments to have fun with Maria. And these options aren't mutually exclusive! But it does warrant noting the lack of women in the development of a story that pivots so heavily on female characters. For all its criticisms of male power fantasies, we still play *Silent Hill 2* from the perspective of men.

Maria once again becomes helpless in the hospital, which, it should be noted, features the game's other sexualized character type: the famous Bubble Head nurses. Buxom and faceless, they've become one of the few monsters to appear in almost every game throughout the rest of the series. They've also, for better or worse, been a focal point of the series's marketing and merchandise. In his book *Silent Hill: The Terror Engine*, Bernard Perron refers to "the penetrating, sped-up respiration" of the nurses, their jerky movements matched with their conventionally attractive body itself a frightening, mutated expression of sexuality.

There's an interesting twist to the hospital. In the same space James is encountering hot zombie nurses, Maria suddenly gets sick and leaves the player behind. At this point in the game, we know next to nothing about James's wife's illness—but we do know it supposedly killed her. In the hospital, Maria's vibrancy is drained. James's implied sexual frustration through his wife's disease is projected onto faceless, aggressive, sexually suggestive enemies while Maria withers.

The time you spend with Maria and the amount of times you check in on her at the hospital can affect the game's ending. The game offers absolutely no hint of this; Maria never asks you to stay. The game doesn't lock you in the hospital until you visit her. As gamers, we're conditioned to believe that a cutscene is separate from the game itself—if there isn't mission data in the scene, we don't need to know anything else. While most games would have a major key moment on which an ending pivots (such as the torture scene in *Metal Gear Solid*), with *Silent Hill 2*, it's the little things that haunt your future.

The loop between gaining and losing Maria continues after a boss fight in the hospital. Once more, James finds Maria. Once more, he confuses her for his late wife, Mary. And once more, Maria mocks James. Eventually the two wind up being chased by Pyramid Head, who seemingly kills Maria. Here James finally shows some real emotion—a scream.

This reaction to Maria's death seems to be one of the few things that pull James out of his confused, muted state. As Perron points out, even the visual and audio framing of the game changes in the moment: "James's panic in front of the closed elevator doors is sharpened by the shaky camera and the closed framing over his shoulder. When an ear-splitting noise shifts to a tearful piano melody after Maria has been stabbed and killed behind the doors, it is hard to struggle against the sadness."

James only feels once he loses a partner. While Maria is alive and healthy, James is distracted and wary. But the moment Maria goes away, *that's* when James cares the most. It's his marriage to Mary all over again.

And then… we're back playing the same game we've been playing for hours. Think about this on a metanarrative level. James just witnessed the murder of a woman who we're supposed to believe has some connection to his wife. He also failed to save her, just like he failed to save Mary. And what does James do? He stands up and… keeps checking those doors. Minutes before, Maria accused James of only caring about his quest to find Mary. And after seeing her killed, he blankly continues his quest with only the briefest of moments of mourning. The adventure continues.

James himself acknowledges this after leaving the hospital, flatly thinking, "Maria's dead. I couldn't protect her. Once again, I couldn't do anything to help. Laura has run off somewhere. Mary… What… What should I do? Are you… really waiting somewhere for me? Or is this your way of taking… I'm going to find Mary… It's the only thing I have left to hope for."

The moment Maria is lost, Mary becomes "active" in James's mind. We as players make the same switch. While we escort Maria, we as players believe that protecting Maria is the most important thing in the world. After all, if she dies, the game is over. However, once she's gone, we're back on our main quest to find Mary. We don't even notice a tension between James's objectives and our own because they're sandwiched by cutscenes that string us along.

Speaking of which, we're intended to think Maria is dead until, *surprise!*, James stumbles upon her alive in a prison cell in the Silent Hill Historical Society. Why is Maria alive and just how did she get into a physical space which shouldn't exist?

Maria calmly tells James that he must be confused about her previous death and is possibly mixing her up with someone else. This gaslighting is ironic as James has spent the entire game confusing Maria for Mary and lying to himself about what happened to his wife. In this scene, James is relieved and happy to see Maria as herself.

And that's when Maria turns on him.

Maria begins remembering things that only Mary could know. "Remember that time in the hotel… You said you took everything… But you forgot that video-tape we made. I wonder if it's still there…" Obviously, we're supposed to believe this is a sex tape James made with Mary. It's also one of the few times in the game that sex is implied in an adult, consensual way, rather than an act of abuse. Sadly, as James is horrified to discover in the hotel, that tape she's describing is footage of him killing his wife. It's a recurring theme in the game: Sexual gratification conflated with violence.

The scene's tone shifts from moment to moment, and ironically, the more Maria returns to her regular, sexual self, the less emotionally invested James becomes. Maria invites James to, "Come and get me. I can't do anything through these bars."

It's hard to tell if Maria is offering James sex in exchange for him to "come and get" her. It's also impossible to tell whether or not James is actually agreeing. James says he "doesn't know" if he wants to touch her. He's dividing Maria from Mary, even as Maria and Mary seem to be merging together.

Once James gets around to opening that jail cell, Maria is dead again. James—true to his character—quietly whines about Maria, again calling her "Mary."

Here's the problem with these scenes: Maria has died before. How are we, or James, supposed to take this? It's hard to be worried about Maria if we know that she'll come back a few scenes later to taunt James. There's a sense that this cycle is James's real punishment, not the busywork of fighting monsters.

In one scene towards the end of the game, James finds Maria hung from a rack flanked by two Pyramid Heads. As James says, "I was weak. That's why I needed you... Needed someone to punish me for my sins... But that's all over now... I know the truth... Now it's time to end this." If James wants to be punished for what he did—then Maria really is "Born from a Wish," as her solo chapter title suggests.

James at last owns up to his crime and accepts culpability in the scene with the two Pyramid Heads in the hotel, saying, "I know the truth… Now it's time to end this." But this realization comes far too late, because one way or another the player must kill a version of Mary.

Sure, if you follow a walkthrough, you can play the game in a manner that gets your desired ending. But inside the game itself, James is never overtly given the option between Mary or Maria. If anything—and to players who don't have a guide handy—the decision between Mary and Maria is completely subconscious.

Silent Hill 2's main campaign sets the player up to read Maria as only existing to haunt James. Her personality is all over the map, her function within the gameplay is limited, and she seems to only be there to drive the narrative forward. But the main quest of the game itself doesn't give much thought to *what* Maria is. James may be an unreliable narrator, but his perspective is the one we're stuck with. If he can't get past the fact that Maria is Mary, we can't get past the fact that Maria is Mary.

This changes quite a bit in "Born from a Wish."

"Born from a Wish" complicates the original *Silent Hill 2* by giving Maria agency she never had before. The fact that we play as her moves Maria from mysterious objectified damsel to protagonist with her own defined inner struggle.

Maria wakes up in a small, claustrophobic room. She wonders how she got there, why no one's around, and whether or not the monsters outside are to blame. She's also got a gun, which is a weird thing to wake up holding. Maria says to herself (or, in a more meta sense, the player) she doesn't have any reason to go on living, but expresses a fear of dying. People in Silent Hill talk like they're just waking up from a long Ambien nap.

When we first meet Maria in the original game, she's confident and cognizant of her surroundings. Here, Maria doesn't even know why she exists. We soon learn Maria was born in Silent Hill—seemingly more of an explanation of her foggy memory than a comfort. Maria isn't in the town to be punished for her sins; she's as much a part of Silent Hill as the monsters.

Maria immediately struggles against suicidal ideations, wanting to die but not wanting to feel the pain of death. As a diagnosed depressive (Hi!), this is an all-too-familiar feeling. Her anxiety over suffering causes her to perpetuate that suffering. Her co-dependent need for a partner is a side effect of this—she needs James so she has a reason to exist. Maria's mental illness reflects Mary's terminal illness: Both need James for support and both are failed by James in that regard.

It's also important that Maria's starting place is the dressing room of Heaven's Night, Silent Hill's tiny, garish strip club where the original game hints that Maria works. The fact that she suddenly becomes aware in Heaven's Night tells us the town is assigning her a role embodying sexuality. Yet in "Born from a Wish," Maria ironically seems anything but sexual.

Maria doesn't want to find a sexual partner. She wants to find *anyone* so she's not alone. Perhaps one could be seen as a surrogate for another, but the difference remains. Who Maria is and what Maria wants are similar, but don't quite line up.

So, let's ask again: What is Maria? Why does her story seem to only revolve around James while the other main characters have their own full, tragic backgrounds? And if she's a punishment designed to lure James into more psychological traps, why do monsters also attack her in "Born from a Wish"? James protecting her in the main campaign makes sense—he's fulfilling the fantasy of being the hero. But if Maria is made by Silent Hill, what is the utility of her being attacked by the town when she's on her own?

Later on, Maria finds a teddy bear. She comments that Laura would love it and then realizes with surprise that she has no idea who Laura is. Maria has Mary's memories; she remembers the little girl she wanted to adopt. But those memories are confused and muddled. Maria *is* Mary, but doesn't know it yet.

"Born from a Wish" comes closest to answering these questions when Maria meets a strange man named Ernest Baldwin. Notably, Baldwin only speaks to Maria through the bedroom door of his large house. As you might expect in a town where nothing normal happens, Baldwin is only asking for help with the simple task of resurrecting his dead daughter, an eerie reflection of James's own quest to find Mary. Yet Maria is expected to help with both.

Baldwin talks about the "Gods"—one way of narrowly tying *Silent Hill 2* to *Silent Hill*. He explains that Maria is from Silent Hill, something he also would definitely *not* have known without a supernatural connection. He also tells her that James is "a bad man," to which Maria responds with a vague, "Y-yes… I know." It would seem that Baldwin isn't giving Maria new information so much as jogging her foggy memory.

Once Maria finally enters Baldwin's room, she encounters no one at all. It's empty, haunted by another ghost of another person with another tragedy. Maria exits the house and, in one of the more troubling scenes in the entire game, quietly ponders killing herself. Then Maria drops her gun, whispers, "James," and walks into the fog.

Maria is a fantasy *and* a punishment. She oscillates between having a death wish and refusing to die. She is killed again and again, each time coming back to life. Maria suffers in her existence. If she's a manifestation of Mary designed to hurt James, she still seems to hold many of the memories and feelings that Mary had for him. Maria may be here to punish James, but she also needs him.

If indeed Maria is "Born from a Wish", it's worth asking—*whose wish*? It's easy to put it on James; he killed Mary and, after all, Maria is everything Mary couldn't be when she was sick. But what if the wish for Maria is Mary's?

In most endings of the game, we learn that Mary's letter was both much longer than we originally knew as well as written before her death. It wasn't an invite; it was a memento. In the letter, Mary apologizes to James: "These last few years since I became ill… I'm so sorry for what I did to you, did to us…" Yet she also worries that James doesn't want her anymore due to her illness and anger: "I wish I could change that, but I can't. I feel so pathetic and ugly laying here, waiting for you…"

Jonathan Barkan of Bloody Disgusting writes, "As much as Silent Hill takes away, it can also give back. I believe that the town and Mary felt both rage and sadness at James and the actions he took at Brookhaven Hospital. For all the violence thrown at James, Mary ultimately gave him someone that he wanted. Even in death, she sent her love."

Maria exists *around* the tragedy of James's game rather than *within* it. She's an avatar of the town—she works there, she lives there, and we find out she's "from" there. She was created by Silent Hill for James. But the choice of whether that means she's a punishment or a reward is tragically taken out of her hands.

ANGELA DID
NOTHING WRONG

FAIR WARNING, THIS CHAPTER is going to deal with physical, emotional, and sexual abuse. If you feel the need to skip this chapter due to this discussion, please do.

Let's start with some real shit: I was abused as a child.

I've spoken about dealing with family violence and bullying in my past, but I was also sexually abused by a neighbor when I was extremely young. I'd rather not go into detail—not because the details are so horrific but because, honestly, it's just a bummer. Nor do I mean to leave it to the imagination to imply it was "worse" than it actually was. It just was something that happened. One of my childhood friends' fathers wasn't a great guy. I hear he's dead now. Shrug emoji.

My generation was warned about "stranger danger." We were told that strangers everywhere wanted to steal us. The most dangerous person in the world was someone we didn't know—usually drawn with an overcoat and sunglasses like they're giving secrets to the government.

We weren't warned about the people we knew outside of very special episodes of sitcoms.

And then it happens.

You question yourself. You tell yourself it wasn't that bad. Later on, you won't confront it because other people have had it worse. You fear that other people who talk about abuse are brave, while if *you* talk about abuse, you're just seeking attention.

You don't tell your family because you don't want that to be how they see you—or for them to pepper you with questions as if the abuse is something you need to relive and prove. You're worried it'll make them feel bad. You're worried they'll secretly tell each other you must be remembering wrong. You feel bad. You feel bad for feeling bad. You feel bad for feeling bad about feeling bad.

Imagine that emotion has been turned into a physical place. A physical manifestation of not just the abuse itself, but also the ways in which you doubt yourself and lash out at others because of that abuse. A place where you could relive your trauma and push back against it, getting caught deeper and deeper as you go.

With its confining geography and enemies matched to traumas, that's what the town of Silent Hill does to its visitors. And of all of those characters, Angela Orosco is easily the most tragic.

James first stumbles upon Angela early in the game while walking through the graveyard. In fact, she's the first non-player character we meet. While we later learn Angela is a teenage runaway, her design and voice acting feel far more adult. During my first playthrough, when I first heard her speak, I genuinely thought Angela was my mom's age. Perron notes in *The Terror Engine* that Sato designed side characters such as Angela to automatically "read" a personality, adding that he wanted to make Angela "look older."

Angela's discomfort is revealed early on while trying to convince James that Silent Hill is dangerous.

> Angela: I think you'd better stay away. This uh... this town... there's something "wrong" with it. It's kind of hard to explain, but...
>
> James: Is it dangerous?
>
> Angela: Maybe... And not just the fog either... It's...
>
> James: Okay, I got it. I'll be careful.
>
> Angela: I'm not lying.

As is par for the course in human existence, victims of abuse often face the secondary trauma of not being believed. James, for his part, is just desperate to find his wife. Angela internalizes his anxiety and lashes out at him. In ignoring Angela's pleas, James takes on the role of abuser by proxy.

This conversation is bizarre on a first playthrough. Both characters seem cagey and confused, the voice acting elevating the game's sense of unreality. Angela sounds out of time and place, while James is oblivious. Neither is capable of listening to the other, and both seem vaguely disturbed by the other's presence. Angela is looking for her mother in a graveyard, James is looking for his wife in a dead town, and neither seems capable of helping the other.

Angela is also being affected by the town. Her expressions are as muted as her clothing—loose pants and layers of sweaters covering almost her entire body. We get the impression Angela does not want to be seen or noticed. Tarrah Rivard, in an article for Rely on Horror, had this to say about the characterization:

> Representatives from Konami insist that Angela's character was only supposed to be 15 or 16 years old. However Donna Burke, the voice actor for Angela Orosco didn't quite fit the bill of a teenager. Angela's official age is 19, but if you've ever heard her voice she still sounds to be in her late 20s or early 30s. It adds a lot of depth to the idea that she is traumatized.

In games such as *Resident Evil*, the awkwardness of the voice acting feels like a bug rather than a feature. True, it adds a B-movie element to proceedings, because—come on—calling a character "the master of unlocking" is hilarious. *Resident Evil*, for all its monsters and mad scientists, takes place in the "real world." Poor voice acting breaks the reality of the moment.

In *Silent Hill 2*, however, the awkward acting *adds* to the atmosphere. We're not in the real world, and the characters don't talk like it. Going by the high definition remaster attempting to "re-do" the acting, it's possible that this isn't intentional. But with the original acting, it's hard to deny the sense of loss we feel as Angela scrounges around a grave, trying to find her mother.

If Angela's trauma makes her shrink from James, it ironically makes James dismiss her advice. Compare this to just a little later in the game when James meets the overtly sexual, more confident Maria. He immediately listens and joins her "quest." Meanwhile Angela, a deeply hurt teenager, gets ignored.

This pattern repeats itself the next time we see Angela in the apartments. She's on the floor, holding a knife, and staring at herself in a mirror. James, assuming Angela is going to kill herself, tells her "there's always another way." Angela says: "Really? But… You're the same as me. It's easier just to run. Besides, it's what we deserve."

It's what we deserve.

The easy and partially correct interpretation is the most obvious one: Everyone in Silent Hill did something wrong. There's an original sin that lands you there, doomed to suffer for all eternity. They "deserve" it.

But it also describes the sense of shame and self-hatred that stems from abuse. Angela isn't sad—she's suicidal. The mirror symbolizes Angela turning inward as she contemplates the value of her own life. She blames herself. The game lets us assume that Angela's search for her mother must parallel James's search for his wife—and if she deserves to suffer, that means James does too.

Angela refuses James's help, but does offer him her knife, saying, "If I kept it… I'm not sure what I might do." However, when James reaches out to take it from her, Angela screams and waves the knife at James saying, "No! I'm sorry… I've been bad… Please don't…" She then leaves the knife behind and exits.

Here Angela oscillates between self-condemnation and self-preservation. She both offers James the knife and waves it at him to keep him from getting too close. Angela is damaged in a very different way than James, her experiences in the town different than his own. They both deserve the same day of reckoning, but they don't deserve the *same* day of reckoning.

You can't help but wonder, "What happened to her?"

Angela doesn't just have trust issues—she doesn't even know how to trust when she wants to. As Kirkland writes in "Gothic Videogames, Survival Horror, and the *Silent Hill* Series": "Across the Silent Hill series, snapshots of traumatic events experienced by playable protagonists, existing outside of interactive space, erupt suddenly and beyond the player's control, disappearing once they have run their course."

This reaction isn't unique to Silent Hill. Victims of sexual assault often have trouble connecting. In a study of the emotional experiences of sexual assault victims, University of Illinois researchers Sarah E. Ullman, Liana C. Peter-Hagene, and Mark Relyea found that:

> Maladaptive coping strategies are cognitive and behavioral strategies that alleviate distress without actually addressing the source of distress itself. These strategies can include cognitive disengagement (e.g., blocking out thoughts), behavioral disengagement (e.g., social withdrawal), denial, and/or use of substances to cope.

We don't learn more about Angela again until we're in the Labyrinth, another location—much like the prison we find Maria in earlier—deep under the Silent Hill Historical Society. We find a bloody newspaper that tells of a "Thomas Oro__." The other letters are missing, as are some throughout the article. In it we learn he was stabbed to death, with police believing it was a "crime o[f pass]ion" (missing letters added) connected to a history of violence and alcoholism. If we've read a website or guide or the manual, we know that "Oro" are the first letters in Angela's last name: Orosco.

It gets worse. As we walk further through the corridors, we hear Angela scream, "No daddy! Please! Don't!"

Even without entering the room, the sound alone paints a horrible picture. Culturally, "daddy" exists in a strange nexus between sexual fetishization and childhood affection. It's a term used in consensual sex play to imply a fantasy power dynamic. The key word here, of course, being "consensual."

Upon entering, we find Angela cowering in the corner of a strange room. The walls are covered in flesh, with orifice-like holes filled with pumping pistons. You get the idea. Opposite Angela is the Abstract Daddy, a fleshy human-like monster merged with a bed. It's a creepy image, an externalization of the way a child views their victimhood. Angela can't separate her father from the bed itself—the person, the act, and the place become one.

Naturally, this horrifying image of tragic innocence lost turns into a standard boss fight.

Despite its grotesque presence, the battle with Abstract Daddy is relatively boring. Run to one side of the room, blast away, run to the other side of the room, blast away again. The game isn't interested in challenging the player; the focus seems to be on the imagery and scene instead of the combat. And when you defeat the Abstract Daddy, Angela is the one to deliver the killing blow by kicking him and dropping a television on his head. As with much of the game, power is taken away from James right when he should feel most victorious.

Curiously, James tells Angela to relax, raising the question, "Who the hell could relax right now?" Throughout the whole game, we're on edge. Anticipating monsters around every corner, we wait to be grabbed, groped, and vomited upon. But the moment Angela does something proactive, James acts as if she's overreacting. Dropping a TV on the head of a monster based on your own sexual abuse isn't overreacting. In fact, it's probably the right amount of reacting.

Angela responds to James, saying, "Don't order me around!" In Angela's moment of triumph—defeating an externalization image of her father—she's silenced by James.

She then delivers one of the most heartbreaking lines in the game: "So what do you want then? Oh I see, you're trying to be nice to me, right? I know what you're up to. It's always the same. You're only after one thing... You don't have to lie. Go ahead and say it. Or you could just force me. Beat me up like he always did." As easy as it may seem to dismiss these accusations, James himself isn't free from sin. Angela isn't being irrational, she's recognizing patterns.

Most action-adventure games "reward" you after a major victory. You might power up. Get a new weapon. Or even get a kiss from the princess. In this instance, the damsel doesn't want to be saved by you. She's suspicious of your motives. The power fantasy withers. Angela isn't here for us, and we're not here for Angela. Just as Angela dropping the TV on the Abstract Daddy kills James's masculine power fantasy, James saving her without her permission steals Angela's agency.

The last time we see Angela, we find her standing on a burning stairwell in the hotel towards the end of the game. The walls of the stairwell are covered with paintings made of sewn-together flesh, with what appear to be mutilated, blood-stained crotches. I never said the Silent Hill games are subtle.

Angela mistakes James for her mother, touching his face in confusion. Angela says, "Mama! Mama, I was looking for you. Now you're the only one left. Maybe then... Maybe then I can rest." Once she realizes James isn't her mother, Angela's tone shifts. "Thank you for saving me... But I wish you hadn't. Even Mama said it... I deserved what happened..." James tells her it's not her fault, to which Angela responds, "No. Don't pity me. I'm not worth it... Or maybe you think you can save me? Will you love me? Take care of me? Heal all my pain?"

We've spent so much time following James and getting to know his suffering that we didn't consider that other characters might be hurting *even more*. In games, non-player characters typically flesh out the world *our* hero is in and drive *our* narrative forward. Here, James's story is secondary to Angela's. The only role James seems to play in Angela's life is doing something for her *she did not want*. All the heroics in the world won't solve her abuse.

There was no person in Angela's life who gave her comfort. Angela may sound excited when she confuses James for her mother, but she's also holding a knife. She says, "Now that you're the only one left. Maybe then… Maybe then I can rest." If she destroys her final abuser, perhaps she can be at peace. Yet we first met Angela looking for her mother in a graveyard. Even with her abusers dead, Angela sees their faces everywhere. Her victimhood doesn't end with her revenge. The trauma is too deep.

And let's talk about the "decor" of this scene. Acknowledging the fire, James says, "It's hot as hell in here," to which Angela responds, "You see it too? For me, it's always like this." Surprise: James and Angela's Otherworlds are different. They may run a parallel path and be in the same physical space, but what they see is usually not the same. With its fire and red color palette, this scene is the one that most resembles the Otherworld of the original *Silent Hill*, and the closest visual reference we've had to the traditional view of Hell: flesh and fire.

When Angela finally exits up the burning stairs, we can't follow. The game won't let us. We have to turn around and exit our own way, and return to our wet, rotting hotel, leaving her to her unknown fate. As a character, she exists outside of James's experiences and is almost entirely unaffected by them. Saving Angela does not save Angela.

It all raises a rather mercenary question: What is Angela's purpose in the game's critical path? What does Angela do for *us* as the player character? On a game level, not much. We get a knife from her, which I guess is cool. But on a narrative level, Angela shows us that James can't be the traditional hero we want him to be. He can't run into the fire and bring her out. You can't solve abuse with a lead pipe.

Angela's story is tragic, but her ascent up those fiery stairs to a place we can't follow means that it is *her* story. Whether she needs or wants James's help is irrelevant. She feels a sense of peace—almost acceptance—as she walks up those stairs. What happened to her can never be erased, but she can take back control. What happens after she walks up those stairs isn't for us.

But James, well, he still has a long way to go.

FATTY FALLS DOWN

Since we're getting to know each other, let me throw out something less sad than the last chapter, but still with a little bit of the old trauma: I was bullied as a kid for being fat. I was a fat kid.

Hell, for a while I was *the* fat kid.

You know the fat kid. They always play the same role in every movie: Lovable side characters entirely defined by their size and the awkwardness that comes with it. In kids' sports movies, they huff as they run down the field. In comedies, they're the best friend who screams at the top of their lungs while diving into a pie. As Chris Farley said, "When fatty falls down everybody goes home happy."

It's a real mixed message when you're the fat kid. On one hand, you get mocked, prodded, and punched for your size. On the other hand, you have a place. You may be fat, and you may be laughed at, but you're being seen. "I'm a garbage bag! Yay!"

Even unintentional humiliations abounded when I was a kid. I had a completely round body and a mass of curly hair. People accidentally called me "ma'am" in stores. My nickname in middle school was "It's Pat!", after the does-not-hold-up-well *SNL* sketch about an androgynous coworker in an office.

I tried to take it all in good fun, until I couldn't. One time a kid went too far and I snapped. I gave it my sad fighting best, attempting to pummel him with sweaty, chubby rage. We were fine, we were bruised up, and it ended. I'm not saying I won the fight, because I didn't. I lost that fight. I lost it bad. But what I remember was how *good* it felt to snap and lash out.

All of which brings me to the character Eddie Dombrowski. Angry, overweight, bullied Eddie. The only non-monster character you fight in the game.

I was Eddie Dombrowski, all the way down to what I wore and how I carried myself. Broad blue and white stripes to hide my stomach. Loose shorts because pants are uncomfortable. Seemingly mismatched socks, one higher than the other. Wide smile that turns into a sneer the moment he feels judged.

Eddie is a caricature of the rage inside every bullied kid. He's a power fantasy of revenge gone wrong. He's the voice in the back of your head saying, "Someday I'll make them all pay. Then they'll be sorry." As Bernard Perron notes in *The Terror Engine*, Eddie's "facial emotion that seems a little bit uncomfortable, [… his] wider pupils, his eyes looking in two directions, one moving a little fast compared to the other." He looks on edge, always ready to attack.

But Eddie is also the only thing approaching comic relief in the game. Even while we witness his anger, see his rage, and eventually kill him in a boss battle, we can *never quite* take him seriously. In a game as intense as *Silent Hill 2*, Eddie is still ridiculous—just as people often find real life analogues of Eddie ridiculous.

We initially run into Eddie in Room 101 of the Woodside Apartments. James discovers a dead body in the kitchen, causing him to ask "What the…? Who could have done this…?" We hear the sound of someone vomiting elsewhere in the apartment and find Eddie in the bathroom. At this point, we've already encountered the "Lying Figure," a straitjacket-like monster that vomits a mist at James. This is what Inger Ekman and Petri Lankoski mean when they talk about the fear of "contamination" in Silent Hill. Monsters seem physically ill, Mary has a mysterious disease, and Eddie pukes.

Besides vomiting, Eddie's first response to the horrors of Silent Hill seems to be deflecting blame. It doesn't matter that there are dead bodies in the building, what matters is that it's not his fault.

Eddie: It wasn't me! I didn't do it!

James: Do what?

Eddie: I didn't do anything. I, I swear! He was like this when I got here...

James: My uh, my name's James. James Sunderland.

Eddie: Ummm... Eddie.

Eddie is defensive before we even know his name. So defensive that James immediately asks, "Eddie, who's that dead guy in the kitchen?" to which Eddie responds, "I didn't do it. I swear I didn't kill anybody."

Eddie may be freaked out by his surroundings—hence the vomiting—but he's far more worried about the prospect of being judged. As we find out later in the game, Eddie does *not* like being criticized; it's a massive trigger for his violent behavior. Because, after all, being unfairly judged is at the core of being bullied.

Of course, we don't know that Eddie was bullied yet at this point. His defensiveness sets us on uneven footing—somewhat similar to Angela's graveyard declaration that "I'm not lying!" Yet there is an important difference: Angela fears not being believed, while Eddie fears being blamed.

Yet he protests a bit too much for our comfort. The more Eddie wants to be normal, the more he becomes an "other" to the audience. In dramatic denial, he is more conspicuous.

The scene continues with James asking perhaps the funniest question in the entire game: "You're not friends with that red pyramid thing, are you?" Which, look, James—probably not. Eddie doesn't seem like the type of person who has *normal* friends, let alone seven-foot-tall monsters with giant swords. They don't hang.

Eddie says, "Red pyramid thing? I don't know what yer talkin' about. Honest. But I did see some weird-lookin' monsters. They scared the hell outta me, so I ran in here…" It fits what we've seen so far, but Eddie still seems suspect. Yes, yes, everyone in Silent Hill has a secret. But Eddie is somehow more self-aware—he lacks Angela's foggy mental state.

Even at this early scene, we *judge* Eddie without even knowing him. With his vomit and his whining, he cuts a disgusting, pitiful figure. It's a relief to get away from him. The fact that James asks him if he's "friends" with Pyramid Head is laughable, but assigns Eddie the role of the "other," or even a potential enemy—which he is. Angela's search for her mother leaves us sympathetic, while Eddie's search for not taking the blame obviously does not.

Eddie's next scene leans even harder into making him seem like a weirdo. This encounter starts with Eddie at the bowling alley talking to our favorite mysterious child, Laura. Eddie, an overweight cartoon of a man, stuffing his face with pizza, brags about fleeing the police. Laura calls him a "gutless fatso" for not owning up to his unspecified crimes and seeking forgiveness. "It's no good," Eddie says. "They wouldn't listen. Nobody will ever forgive me."

There's so much to discomfort us in this scene.

First of all, where in God's name did Eddie get fast food in Silent Hill? As James says, "This town is full of monsters! How can you sit there and eat pizza?" Did the town manifest a pizza for Eddie to make him feel bad about his body? Later, in the prison, we'll find a grave for Eddie marked "Gluttonous Pig." If his trauma comes from body shaming, it's ironic the town would have readily available junk food. Silent Hill perpetuates the cycle.

Second, we should be concerned that a grown man is hanging out with a random little girl, right? It's a massive red flag. For a game rife with imagery of sexual trauma, Eddie and Laura's relationship makes us immediately uncomfortable.

Yet Laura bullies Eddie. She's cruel. She may be small, but her attacks give her a higher status. For his part, Eddie is so desperate for approval that he tries to impress a child with his criminal cred. Even in a place where his life is in danger, all Eddie cares about is what others think of him. With James, Eddie professes innocence of any crime—he's just a guy who happens to be in Silent Hill. With Laura, Eddie seems to exaggerate his own criminal exploits. Watch out: We've got a badass over here!

This would all seem cruel if Eddie himself didn't twist the bullying to his own ends. When Laura calls Eddie a fatso, he bristles. He wants to be more than his body. Yet when James asks Eddie why he won't help Laura, he uses that same bullying to stay put. "She said a fatso like me would just slow her down."

Sure, maybe that's true. Laura, for lack of a better term, is undeniably an asshole. But this fatso is a grown man. And in a town filled with horror, maybe that fatso could try to see past his own self-pity and care about someone else. There's a scolding tone in this response, too. Not only is his bullying a reason to avoid helping, it's a reason to let Laura get hurt. She hurt him, so she deserves to suffer too.

Eddie is a classic bully-victim, which a study published in the journal *School Psychology Quarterly* describes as "someone who bullies and is bullied," and "has negative attitudes and beliefs about himself or herself and others [...]. He or she has trouble with social interaction, does not have good social problem-solving skills, performs poorly academically and is not only rejected and isolated by peers but is also negatively influenced by the peers with whom he or she interacts."

The qualities that made Eddie a victim also make us dislike Eddie, which further makes Eddie a victim, which further makes him respond in a way we find off-putting.

Eddie constantly talks down about himself, yet when others respond with the same criticism, he lashes out. He can't connect with the people he meets in Silent Hill because he projects his insecurities onto them in a cycle of blame and isolation. The fact that we as players ultimately have to kill Eddie only confirms his paranoia that we're judging him. It may be a self-fulfilling prophecy, but it's also one we willingly participate in.

This is Eddie's punishment.

Every other character in the game is seeking someone, seeking a connection to deal with the past. Angela wants her mother. James and Laura want Mary. Maria wants James. They want *someone*. Eddie, however, wants to be left alone with his pizza. He didn't come to Silent Hill to find something: In his own words, he "ran 'cause [he] was scared."

We may encounter monsters, but Eddie encounters something even worse: other people. Jean-Paul Sartre says hello.

Unfortunately for Eddie, James runs into him two more times in short succession—and guess what? Both are food-related. As you might expect based on our experiences with everyone else in the game, we run into Eddie in the Silent Hill Historical Society. Apparently the "historical" part of the name also refers to the characters themselves. And do we ever learn about Eddie's history.

Here, we find Eddie in what seems to be a cafeteria. As with his first appearance in the apartments, Eddie is near a corpse that he may or may not have killed.

Eddie: Killin' a person ain't no big deal. Just put the gun to their head... Pow!

James: You... you killed him.

Eddie: B-but... it wasn't my fault. He, he made me do it!

James: Calm down, Eddie. Tell me what happened.

Eddie: That guy... he, he had it coming! I didn't do anything. He just came after me! Besides he was making fun of me with his eyes! Like that other one...

James: Just for that you killed him.

Eddie: Whaddaya mean "Just for that"!?

James: Eddie, you can't just kill someone cause of the way they looked at you...

Eddie: Oh yeah! Why not? 'Til now I

always let people walk all over me. Just like
that stupid dog. He had it coming too!!

Eddie brags, then immediately denies he killed the
man, then says he was only joking, and then runs off
deeper into the Silent Hill Historical Society. He wants
to seem masculine to James—but he also doesn't want
to be judged. And to be fair, it's hard to know whether
or not Eddie actually killed the man in the cafeteria—
there are a lot of bodies scattered around Silent Hill. It's
certainly possible he killed some, but we don't see it.
Plus, as we saw in the bowling alley, Eddie is super lazy.
He doesn't really have the commitment of a serial killer.

Eddie's tonal shift between the past and the present is also troubling. His focus suddenly shifts to who
he's hurt in the past: "that other one," the person who
bullied him, and "that stupid dog," which was, well, a
dog. Eddie can't help but switch back and forth between
insecurities. He wants to be liked and feared in equal
measure. "I didn't do anything" turns into "He had it
coming too!"

Soon we have our final encounter with Eddie in a meat
freezer. One last time, we're given food-related scenery for
the man who was bullied for his body. This isn't a coincidence. Eddie's trauma stems from his awkward body. His
Silent Hill surroundings always emphasize his obesity. The
hanging meat is a play on the "pig" designation given to

Eddie by the town. At the very end, Eddie has to confront the way he thinks everyone sees him.

If he was on the precipice of insanity before, this is him taking a full dive.

Eddie monologues about the way people view him and his physical appearance. He quotes the insults he's weathered over the years: "You fat disgusting piece of shit!" and "Fat-ass, yer nothin' but a waste of skin." But he doesn't completely disagree, either. "Well maybe he was right. Maybe I am nothing but a fat, disgusting piece of shit. But ya know what? It doesn't matter if you're smart, dumb, ugly, pretty… it's all the same once yer dead. And a corpse can't laugh."

Too bad Eddie thinks everyone is laughing at him. As he explains to James:

> Do you know what it does to you, James? When you're hated, picked on, spit on, just cause of the way you look. After you've been laughed at your whole friggin' life. That's why I ran away after I killed the dog. Ran away like a scared little girl. Yeah, I killed that dog. It was fun. It tried to chew its own guts out! Finally died all curled up in a ball. Then *he* came after me, I shot him too. Right in the leg. He cried more than the

dog! He's gonna have a hard time playing football on what's left of that knee.

James tells Eddie that he needs help because "You think it's okay to kill people." To which Eddie responds that him and James are the same. Eddie may be in a paranoid delusion, but then again, all of Silent Hill *is* a paranoid delusion. James wouldn't be in Silent Hill if he was an innocent man who did normal things with his wife.

Fat, sad Eddie might be a psycho, but he's also right: He and James have both committed violent acts. It forces us to come to a reckoning. Until this point, we've spent every encounter judging Eddie. If not judging him for his appearance, judging him by his bragging, denial, and crazed self-protection. We don't have to have to fight Eddie because we don't like his body, we have to fight Eddie because Eddie assumes that we hate him for his body.

An essay analyzing Eddie on the blog "Of A Sound Mind and Body" addresses this duality:

> Eddie is not visually threatening or scary, the player is meant to be afraid of Eddie's insanity. The way he lies one moment, tells the truth the next, then lies again is where the fear begins. Despite Eddie having been bullied, the player is not meant to feel any sympathy for him, and by the end, the

player is left feeling as though perhaps this bullying was well deserved, walking away from his body without a second thought.

At the end of the day, what did James do? He killed his wife because he couldn't take her sickness anymore. As we later learn in the game, Mary routinely mocked James while he was caring for her. Maybe James didn't like being bullied either, perhaps he reacted in the same manner that Eddie did: violently. James whining, "I killed a... human being" after defeating Eddie in the game only emphasizes the irony.

In a morbid way, Eddie's death should be satisfying for us as players. He's unlikable. He's weird. He attacked James. Putting him down should feel like an event. That's the point of a boss battle, isn't it? Big moments! Triumphing over evil and feeling powerful. But here again, *Silent Hill 2* works hard to subvert masculine power fantasies. It doesn't want you to feel good about killing the baddie. Relieved, maybe. But good? No way.

At that final moment, James acknowledges that Eddie isn't like the other monsters he's faced: Eddie isn't an abstract butcher with a metal head, he's just a sad, damaged man. Killing him feels different from the other encounters we've had in the game because it *is* different. Fatty may fall down, but nobody is laughing.

Eddie Dombrowski is as relatable as he is unlikable. He's the part of us that uses trauma as an excuse to lash out. He was hurt by real people and turned that around to become an abuser himself, reveling in the pain he causes innocent people and animals.

He created monsters so he could fight monsters.

Eddie built his own Silent Hill before he even got there.

DOES PYRAMID HEAD MATTER?

YOU SEE THE NAME OF THE CHAPTER, so let's cut right to it.

Marketing wise, he—if Pyramid Head even is a "he"—definitely matters to Konami. With his bloody butcher's outfit, pointy metal head, and massive sword, Pyramid Head's head looks like the dream of every teenage goth. He's the perfect fit for merchandise: Intimidating and iconic, he's video games' version of horror mainstays like Jason Voorhees from Friday the 13th or Michael Myers from the Halloween movies.

In *Silent Hill 2*, he's also a violent rapist—one that just happens to be available on a shirt and in a kart racing game.

In his first appearance, Pyramid Head is standing on the other side of a passage from James in an apartment building. The passage is blocked off by bars and Pyramid Head himself doesn't react to the player. It's an unsettling sight that reflects what Kevin F. Steinmetz in

"Carceral Horror" calls the "representations of prisons and punishment [that] are evident in many entertainment genres, perhaps the most visceral are found in horror." We can't tell if we're the ones behind bars or he is—are we being protected or trapped?

While many of the enemies in the game tend to crouch into their own bodies and painful shapes as a sign of trauma and pain, Pyramid Head stands tall above James. His calm demeanor draws our focus directly onto him. We wait because we expect him to act. His passivity creeps us out; enemies are made to attack. Instead, he waits—establishing a power dynamic by looking evil and doing, well, absolutely nothing.

This all changes with Pyramid Head's infamous "rape scene." Later in the apartments, James comes across Pyramid Head assaulting two struggling Mannequin enemies. The Mannequin enemies consist of two pairs of plastic, feminine-looking legs stacked on top of each other to form "arms" and "legs" with no head. It's a sexual image, one made only more disturbing when the legs of both halves move.

During this sequence, Pyramid Head corners both Mannequins in the kitchen, seemingly holding one down as he grotesquely thrusts into them. Meanwhile, James hides in a closet like a scared child. But he's also *watching*—especially watching from a place of cliché perversion. Whether or not James is enjoying it, he is watching an assault while we as players lose any control. We can't make James stop the rape. We can't make him turn away.

This moment throws a lot at us. If the game's designers wanted to spook the player, they could have Pyramid Head just chase James down a hallway like they do with most of the other enemies. He could be a direct danger to us. Instead, Pyramid Head violently assaults another monster while we have to do nothing.

In "Gothic Videogames, Survival Horror, and the Silent Hill Series," Kirkland refers to Pyramid Head in this scene as a "castrating father," adding, "The father's assault on the mother is presented in Pyramid Head's introductory cutscene, where he is spied either murdering, raping, or giving birth to a female-coded mannequin creature." His positioning is masculine, his violence against a feminine figure pronounced and out in the open. Pyramid Head openly attacks female bodies, while James hides—both in that closet and from his own violent past.

Sexual violence in horror is obviously nothing new. From *Hellraiser* (1987) to *Se7en* (1995) to *Midsommar* (2019), sexuality and violence are central themes to the genre. In an article for Bust magazine, Rémy Bennett points out that Freddy Krueger of A Nightmare on Elm Street fame—himself a horror movie icon—is entirely centered around sexual violence. "Freddy was a sexual

predator, a rapist and abuser of children, a taker of innocence, a paedophile, and a murderer […] 'Elm Street' is
code for 'Anywhere, USA.'"

Silent Hill, of course, is also code for "Anywhere,
USA"—at least as envisioned by a group of Japanese
developers.

The scene is complicated by the fact that Pyramid
Head's sexual violence takes place against another monster
in the game. Sexual assault alone is dehumanizing. By
presenting the victim as a headless, sexual figure, the act
becomes even more alien. There's a tragedy and pathetic
quality to most of *Silent Hill 2*'s basic enemies. Aimless
and flesh-bound, they're just human enough to feel. We
take on an anxiety that something *happened* to make
them this way, and we might be next. Pyramid Head
shows us that these monsters truly suffer. We hurt them
more with our bag of badass weapons anyway.

Pyramid Head seems to exist in Silent Hill for and
because of James. Each character hints their experience
in the town is different. When James asks Eddie if he's
seen the "red pyramid thing," Eddie doesn't know what
he's talking about. While Eddie is a liar, it's hard to
imagine what he gains from lying about crossing paths
with Pyramid Head.

In fact, James only encounters Pyramid Head alone
or while he's with Maria, who herself exists as part of
James's self-inflicted punishment. But if Pyramid Head

was "created" to punish James, then it raises a lot of questions about its abuse of other enemies in the game—not to mention his phallic head, giant knife, and spear. As Maria's sexualization is representative of James's frustrated desires during Mary's sickness, then Pyramid Head is the flip side of that coin—the rage in James directed at his wife's illness. Whether it was mercy to suffocate her with a pillow, or a selfish act out of sexual and psychological frustration, it's hard to ignore that James wanted something that could only be achieved through violence.

For an example, look no further than the scene in the hospital with James with Maria. Here we've already faced the Bubble Head Nurses standing in for all the women James dealt with in the hospital *while* his wife was sick. To be delicate, it would appear James had weird, scary boners that he had weird, scary pangs of guilt about wherever his wife was incapable of giving him physical attention.

It's also in this hospital that Pyramid Head suddenly appears and kills Maria—permanently taking her away from James (well, for a brief period of time). Right away, there's the body horror of what we've seen Pyramid Head do to enemies in the game. Pyramid Head is thrusting an object into Maria, the monster embodiment of James' desires. In our triangle-faced friend, James's violent sexuality manifests itself as cruel and hurtful, destroying the source of desire.

This carries over to boss fights too. Like much of the combat in Silent Hill, every battle with Pyramid Head is a chase—run to one side of the area, fire some rounds, run away from Pyramid Head's attacks, fire more rounds. Pyramid Head moves with a lazy ease, slowly following James and wildly swinging his knife. When Bernard Perron talks about Pyramid Head in *The Terror Engine*, he focuses on his speed:

> *SH2* is very slow paced. It is not an action-filled package. The monsters are not that numerous and are easily avoided. In fact, *SH2* relies on one of the most essential features of gameplay: time, real time. It is indicative of the way you are made to play the game that you simply can't kill Pyramid Head. You can only endure through enough time to make him leave or kill himself…

The game forces us to savor moments with Pyramid Head. We can't simply own him with the right weapon or the right trick because James doesn't ever actually *beat* Pyramid Head. In their first battle, Pyramid Head seems to grow bored and walk away. Meanwhile our final battle against two Pyramid Heads ends with them both stabbing each other. We may progress in the game, but it doesn't feel like a victory in battle.

YouTuber RagnarRox takes it a step further in his analysis of Pyramid Head. He points out that Pyramid Head is never quite a threat to James, but in fact helps James reach his goal. Even when Pyramid Head knocks James through a fence at the hospital, he does it "deliberately, in a non-lethal manner. He could've easily chopped James to pieces, but instead he just pushes James off the roof with the pommel of his great sword."

Despite his massive presence in the game and merchandising outside of it, Pyramid Head isn't really a "villain" in *Silent Hill 2*. Enemy, yes. But he doesn't appear to have any actual motivations outside of violence and sexual assault. He exists solely to drive James onward to face the horrors of what he wants and what he did.

Then there's Pyramid Head's famous weapon, the "Great Knife." Yes, yes, we've already said it's phallic. But it is interesting that James can find and use it. Hell, it's one of the most powerful weapons in the game! The "Great Knife" is also almost exactly the same in design as the suicide knife given to James by Angela, just ridiculously bigger.

A symbol of sexual assault becomes our most powerful weapon. Through gameplay, the game encourages James to become *more* like Pyramid Head.

Pyramid Head is both a punishment and a form of wish fulfillment for James. He's powerful, he's unstoppable, and he's in control. He may be a monster in Silent Hill, but unlike the other monsters, he doesn't *care* what's happening. He's everything James wanted in that moment he suffocated Mary—the ability to take what he wants through violence, his face covered and his guilt absolved.

James isn't just trapped in Silent Hill, he's drawn to it. He's not trying to "escape" Silent Hill, he's trying to find peace in it through the catharsis of his punishment. Just as we as players aren't booting up a horror game to "stop" the feeling of terror and disgust, but to experience them and revel in them. Pyramid Head is created because of James, not to stop James.

NO HAPPY ENDINGS

LET'S TALK ABOUT VIDEO GAME ENDINGS.

Specifically, video games that have multiple endings. Aren't they wonderful? We get to decide the fates of worlds through every decision. Characters live or die at our behest, with unexpected results shocking and delighting us for hours.

It's exhausting.

Nothing fills me with more dread than the phrase "multiple endings" because I know I'm going to miss something unless I read a damn walkthrough. But walkthroughs basically screw you out of the fun of surprise because they, well, *walk you through it*. My entire world collapses around me as I realize that free will is a myth and choice is a lie and I'm going to do a lot of Googling to get the canonical "true" ending.

Thankfully, *Silent Hill 2* has no "true" ending. It doesn't even have a "good" ending like the original game. As game critic Alexander Kriss puts it,

The clear-cut binary choices that I enjoyed when replaying the first game were gone. In *Silent Hill*, if I used the unknown liquid, Cybil lived and I saw a "plus" ending. Otherwise, she died and I saw a "minus" ending. End of story. [...] It didn't matter how I treated Cybil throughout the game, or how I really felt about her deep down in the inky black of my unconscious. In *Silent Hill 2*? I wasn't so sure.

While the original *Silent Hill*'s endings relied on gameplay choices, they were also easier to figure out. Save a character, get an item, use an item. The game may not have been explicit in these mechanisms, but the link between the actions and the results was clearer.

Silent Hill 2 is far more subtle. Rather than relying on moral "choices" or overt gameplay mechanisms, *Silent Hill 2* gives players endings based on small, unacknowledged decisions. Sercan Şengün refers to this as "invisible agency," writing that, "the ending [the player] achieves may also reflect a psychological profiling for himself."

For the sake of clarity, I'll lay out the three standard endings of *Silent Hill 2* first, followed by the "second playthrough" ending, and then the joke endings last. The joke endings don't really have anything to do with the story of the game, and they're achieved entirely different ways than the first four, so keep in mind you're not missing much by not spending an entire playthrough trying to see a dog programming the game. Although I do have a dorky point to make about it. Buckle up, folks!

If you still haven't played the game, let me recap its final couple of hours: In the hotel, James plays a videotape that forces him to face the fact that he killed his wife. We also learn that Mary had been verbally abusive during her sickness, which itself may or may not have triggered James's violence. A fight with two Pyramid Heads later, we climb a set of stairs to get to the endgame. Got it? Great.

When we reach the top of the hotel, we see a woman who looks like Mary. Not Maria, with her bright clothing and makeup and tattoos but plain old Mary. Here's where things get complicated.

In the ending dubbed "Leave," James calls this woman "Mary," only to have her say, "When will you ever stop making that mistake! Mary's dead. You killed her." James, realizing it's Maria, says he doesn't need her anymore. Maria responds angrily, demanding he love her. "I'll never yell at you or make you feel bad. That's what you wanted. I'm different than Mary… How can you throw me away?" James says it's "time to end this nightmare," to which Maria responds, "No! I won't let you! You deserve to die too, James." She then turns into a monster. It's a monster similar to Abstract Daddy—a human shape seemingly melted into a bed frame. Once more we confront a tragic sexuality.

After killing Maria (a death that's hard to trust considering her in-game deaths and resurrections), the scene suddenly switches to a bedroom. James observes Mary in bed. Mary confesses she wanted to die, implying she wanted James to kill her. James says he did it for her, then confesses that he hated Mary and wanted her out of the way. "I wanted my life back."

Mary, who's in a super good mood apparently, waves off this fucked-up admission and gives James a letter, telling him to move on with his life. Sure. If there's one thing that's been good for James so far, it's getting letters from Mary. Those letters do *real* good work.

It turns out the letter that Mary gives to James is a much longer version of the one that kicked off the game. Here we get a lot of exposition in which Mary apologizes for being hard on James, tells him she loves him, and says, "That's why I want you to live for yourself now. Do what's best for you, James. James... You made me happy."

This letter is played with Mary's narration over a scenic graveyard. As the letter ends, Laura can be seen walking, with James behind her, implying they're both safely leaving Silent Hill together.

To achieve this ending, you're required to keep your health as high as possible at all times, check Mary's photo and letter in your inventory often, spend as little time with Maria as possible, and fully listen to all conversations with Mary in the hotel, rather than ending them early by running into another room.

In other words, to get this ending, James must focus on his health and his wife and while essentially rejecting Maria. As a player, these criteria can come off as unfair and confusing—after all, we're trained to think of most inventory items as directly useful to the immediate present: The letter seems irrelevant so our instinct isn't to repeatedly check it. The same goes for healing. We're accustomed to saving health packs for when we need them, yet if we want this ending, we have to stay as healthy as possible.

Despite Mary's forgiveness, there is something troubling about this ending. While Mary absolves James of any wrongdoing, she is given the voice to do so only *after* she was murdered. And that voice is telling James that everything he did was more or less okay. At the same time, James just suffered through Silent Hill— which means he still, in some way, was being punished. As our final boss, Maria becomes the ultimate creation of James's guilt.

But in killing Mary's doppelgänger, James is still killing a form of Mary. As Ewan Kirkland writes in "Discursively Constructing the Art of Silent Hill": "The ending to *Silent Hill 2* makes player experience the inescapability of James's psychotic obsession with his wife's murder/euthanasia, presenting killing Mary as the only possible action to complete the game." The fact that Mary forgives James before and after her death doesn't mean James can ever completely forgive himself.

The "Leave" ending could be considered the closest to a happy one. But it's too pat, too nice. The wheels come off the story. You're telling me that Angela walks into the flames, Eddie dies, but James just waltzes out of Silent Hill with an adopted daughter and forgiveness in his heart? It seems unlikely. In a normal video game, the uplifting ending is often the canonical one. But here it's out of place. It doesn't fit quite right.

The ending dubbed "In Water" starts off somewhat similar. Again, James confronts Maria at the top of the stairs in the hotel. When he confuses Maria with Mary, she says, "Wrong again. Mary's dead. You killed her." The rest of their dialogue before the battle is pretty much the same, including Maria's transformation. How do you solve a problem like Maria? You blow her away!

Afterward, we come to another scene with Mary in the bedroom. But things play out a bit differently. Rather than forgiving James, Mary says, "You killed me and you're suffering for it. It's enough, James." She's terser, but here again Mary seems to absolve him. He's paid his debt. Mary gives James the same letter as last time, but here she coughs and dies. James then carries her out of the room.

Cut to black. James says he understands the real reason he came to Silent Hill: He wants to be together with Mary. We hear car screeches and then cut to an underwater backdrop with bubbles rising to the surface as Mary narrates the letter. It's dark, even for *Silent Hill 2*.

To get this ending, the player must maintain low health, repeatedly look at Angela's knife in the inventory, read a special diary in the hospital, fully listen to the conversations with Mary, and read an earlier message in a bar that says, "If you really want to see Mary, you should just die. But you might be heading to a different place than Mary, James."

In other words, to get this ending, you need to focus on your own guilt, shame, and death.

It's implied James killed himself by driving his car into the lake *before* the events of the game. This actually makes a lot of sense if we look at the first few minutes of *Silent Hill 2*. James's car is parked askew in front of the lake, he reads only part of the letter asking him to return to Silent Hill, and he starts the game by looking into a reflective surface—you know, like water.

In fact, there's water imagery throughout the game. James crosses a lake, rain pours through the hotel, and rising floods prevent James from going back the way he came. Similar to the ending of *Jacob's Ladder*, it's possible James's Hell is in his mind as he's dying. As life leaves his body, he comes to an understanding with his sins.

Make no mistake, the ending is suicide. Remember that, to get it, you need to focus on the knife Angela gave you. A knife, it's worth remembering, she was going to use to kill herself. The letter itself works as a reverse suicide note—a formal invitation to join Mary in death.

However, James killing himself means that every character is in Hell or, as I believe, existing only in James's head. In this ending, the other characters aren't manifesting their own versions of Silent Hill—they're all manifestations of different aspects of James himself. Eddie becomes James's bullied, masculine rage. Pyramid Head becomes James's sexual violence. Angela becomes James's shame. Laura, James's disappointment in his familial failures. Maria is... still Maria.

A fair number of people consider this the canon ending with good reason. The novelization of the game even uses it. But a novelization of a video game isn't the game, and it would rob *Silent Hill 2* of its emotional weight if *nothing* the player did actually mattered. It's far more intriguing that James's punishment means different things based on how the *player* acts and not how the designers thought James should end up.

It's a compelling final scene, but we still can't assume it's the "true" one.

In a third ending, "Maria," the Mary that James encounters at the top of the stairs is... Mary! That's right, she doesn't transform into Maria. Rather, we get a darker version of the conversation in the previous two endings. James says he wanted to see Mary, "even [as] an illusion." He also tries to say he killed Mary for her own sake (come on, buddy). Mary replies, "Don't make excuses, James. I know I was a burden on you. You must have hated me. That's why you got rid of me." Mary concludes that she can't forgive James for what he did and thus turns into a monster.

So now Mary's the final boss, albeit a final boss that's identical to the others. James has sought Mary throughout this game and now he must fight her. We might tell ourselves at the start that James is here to save Mary, but in our last act as players, we save ourselves *from* Mary. We help James kill his wife a second time. We face the question: Does James ever get to leave Silent Hill, or is this just a cycle of punishment?

After this battle, James is back in the park where he met Maria. Maria opens the conversation with her smoothest line yet: "You killed Mary again?" James confesses that he wants to be with Maria. We get the letter again, this time played over a distant shot of the starting location of the game. As James and Maria walk to her car, Maria coughs and James—hilariously—says, "You'd better do something about that cough."

Got it? We're all clear that she's going to die, right?

Unsurprisingly, this ending is best achieved by protecting Maria and spending as much time as possible with her, including checking on her in the hospital when she gets weak. We also have to ignore and rush through any Mary-related story beats and scenes. In our actions, we must show that Maria is more important to us than Mary.

If you're not playing with a walkthrough, this is by far the most likely ending you'll get in the game. It's definitely the one I first got. Why? Because as gamers, we're trained to protect a non-player character (Maria) in an escort mission. We instinctively care for her because the game asks us to. It isn't a coincidence that Maria is much more of a traditional female video game love interest. She's aggressive and funny and sexual yet regularly needs saving—something that would've been familiar to fans of contemporary games such as *Metal Gear Solid*.

James lives and he gets the girl. Yet her cough leaves us with the knowledge that James (and by extension, us) didn't get what he wanted. We still failed, and we're left with the fear that James will repeat his cycle of violence. He's already killed one ill partner, why not two?

This is why I love Silent Hill 2*!*

In Silent Hill, even good endings have disturbing implications. James can't just walk away from what he did, even when he's basically just walking away from what he did. There's no one choice that makes everything okay, because the most important choice in James's life comes before we even start the game. James can defeat his demons, but he can't leave Hell.

This brings us to the "Rebirth" ending, which can only be achieved on a second playthrough. The penultimate scene at the top of the hotel is similar to "Leave" and "In Water"; Maria is our final boss. However, when we kill her, we don't get Mary's deathbed absolution. Instead, James talks to Mary's corpse while rowing a boat toward a mysterious island.

James says in his flat affectation, "Mary. You look so peaceful. Forgive me for waking you. But without you, I just can't go on. I can't live without you, Mary. This town, Silent Hill... The Old Gods haven't left this place... And they still grant power to those who venerate them... Power to defy even death... Ah... Mary." We then reach an island and fade to black.

To get this ending, you have to collect various odds and ends throughout the game, specifically items that only appear on a second playthrough. Curiously, one of these is the same White Chrism (don't laugh), which was used by Maria to bring back Ernest Baldwin's daughter in "Born from a Wish." Yet the most important thing to remember is that we can only get this ending the second time around. James can only revive his wife—if that's what's going to happen—if he already understands how the town works. Our second playthrough seems to be *his* second playthrough.

This actually fits! The way James talks here is different than the rest of the game. Nowhere else does he mention "The Old Gods," and nowhere else does he have the same confidence that he can save Mary. He *knows* what he's doing.

We're left with two options. One, James knew what was happening all along and—armed with occult knowledge of the gods of the previous Silent Hill game—eagerly walked into the town to get his wife back.

This gives us the badass, guns-a-blazin' hero we never got in our first playthrough of *Silent Hill 2*. On our second playthrough, James isn't lost—he's a man with a plan. Unfortunately, he's also a man who kept his wife's body in the trunk of the car while he acted out that plan.

The other option is that James's punishment repeats itself and James finally "learned" the rules and got out. Think of this as *Groundhog Day*, except it's Hell and instead of falling in love, James learns to appease dark elder gods that can bring back his dead wife. Whom he murdered, let's not forget that. Really a big mulligan to take there.

Personally, I don't accept the "Rebirth" ending as canonical either. It undercuts the mythos set up by the rest of the game. *Silent Hill 2* posits that each of the characters has a "reason" to be in town, a trauma that's being projected. Directly connecting James's story with the cult of the first game takes away so much of the gravity behind his tragedy and that of the other characters in the game. This ending turns his eternal torment into a fun puzzle to be solved.

The "Rebirth" ending also clashes with the "Born from a Wish" segment. Is Maria an obstacle to prevent James from reviving Mary? Is she supposed to be a choice? Was she created by some eldritch gods to test James? Once we move away from the central theme of the rest of the game, the plot becomes a bit cloudy.

One way to consolidate "Rebirth" with the rest of *Silent Hill 2* is to revisit the idea that each other character represents some form of James. Laura, Eddie, and Maria all fit into James's psyche pretty well. The child they never had, the bullied man who lashes out, the ideal version of a partner you let down. This is an imperfect explanation: Angela doesn't quite work.

Angela suffered extreme sexual abuse from her family. Her story doesn't line up with the "Rebirth" ending in any metaphorical way. Perhaps Angela is a representation of James's sexual violence—the silencing of Mary because she was no longer capable of fulfilling his desires. Yet it still feels like a reach when James saves Mary through dark magic. Angela wasn't the perpetrator of abuse, now seeking to turn back the clock, and her familial murders carry some weight of vengeance—something this ending just doesn't have.

Angela and Eddie's stories are compelling; making them all a figment of James's punishment robs the emotional impact of their stories. It's an ending like the one on the television show *St. Elsewhere*, where all the events turned out to be a boy looking into a snow globe. It puts an unsatisfying bow on the experience for the sake of wrapping things up.

The other endings in *Silent Hill 2* are, of course, "Dog" and "UFO." Let's look at those briefly because, why not? We all like to have fun, don't we?

The "Dog" ending, for lack of a better term, is amazing. You can only unlock this ending after getting all three normal endings or the "Rebirth" ending. But unlike the other endings so far, The "Dog" ending doesn't itself require another full playthrough. It still takes some work to achieve it, but it intentionally disconnects itself from the full experience.

Here, James walks into a room filled with monitors and a dog pulling levers. James drops to his knees and says in Japanese, "So it was all your work!" And then… we get an upbeat credits montage. Some pictures in the montage are disturbing, some are weirdly sexy shots of James and Maria, and a few references to Eddie being fat. Yes, fat-shaming is wrong, but in the context of the game, Eddie did kill a dog, so you'd see why the one controlling Silent Hill might not like him. Yes, I'm saying the dog put together the montage. It's my book.

Here's my deep analysis… No, I'm screwing with you. It's fun that takes the piss out of the game. The voice acting isn't even localized—the scene is in Japanese, making it feel all the sillier and less connected to the narrative we've experienced so far. The scene isn't worth translating outside of subtitles because it's not *really* part of the story. But it's not just random humor. It's a response to our desire to know the "true" ending of the game. Is a dog controlling Silent Hill that much crazier than elder gods or externalized shame? No. Well, maybe.

Much like the "Born from a Wish" episode, the "UFO" ending is only available in later releases of *Silent Hill 2*. It's also only unlockable if you've finished both the original game and the aforementioned "Born from a Wish." To unlock it, James must pick up a blue gem in the bathroom at the start of the game and then use it in three other locations.

Once achieved, we see a series of UFOs approach the hotel and a PS1-model of *Silent Hill*'s Harry Mason. Harry talks to James in a black and white, silent film-like scene with the dialogue replaced by title cards. Eventually, aliens zap James and Harry and the aliens kidnap them, leading into equally old-timey credits.

A few narrative twists and this could've been a real ending for the game. The game's designers could easily throw the old *Twilight Zone* "It was an experiment by aliens!" curveball. Seriously, even an appearance by Harry could've been an "Oh, shit!" moment if it were played straight.

The "Dog" and "UFO" endings are clearly rewards for people who invested a lot of time into the game. They also remind the players to not take the game too seriously (or write a 30,000+ word book on it).

It's worth noting that the three endings requiring additional runs feature specific tasks to unlock, while the three that can be found on a first playthrough are decided through minor choices. Without knowing it, the endings the player is most likely to get reflect how we roleplay James.

As Alexander Kriss says, "*Silent Hill 2* refuses to indulge our desire for omnipotence, for carefully planning out each step to willfully steer what happens to us and the broader story. Instead, we make decisions that we think we understand, which may or may not matter, and that yield outcomes at once logical and wholly opaque."

Games such as *Mass Effect* inform us when we've made a clear, morally "positive" or "negative" choice. When we have the option to help a character or rob them, the game and I both know there *is* a choice being made, and we probably also know how it'll affect us. We often even get a little notification when we make a moral choice! It's good to find out we're good!

Instead, *Silent Hill 2*'s changing narrative arc can be observed more in games such as *Undertale*, a roleplaying game in which killing some, killing all, or not killing any enemies directly affects the outcome of the game. This information is only hinted at in dialogue, and the user never receives direct confirmation that their choices are affecting the outcome.

As with much of *Silent Hill 2*, we're left to our own devices. There is no true ending, just the one that interprets how we played the game. If we drown in a car or get the girl, it's because of how we acted as James. There's no true happy ending because there's no way to absolve James for what he's done. The game resists giving us exactly what we want or the tools to even know how to get it, leaving us to interpret our own fate and how we got here.

Or there's a dog.

PLAYING AND
SELLING DREAD

Silent Hill 2 is a very good game.

Silent Hill 2 is not a very fun game.

Its controls are slow, even for its time. It's relatively linear. It's not that challenging, even on higher difficulties. There is no "leveling up" or insane loot for your efforts. Pretty much everything your character can do at the start of the game, he can also do at the end. Even as a horror experience it isn't that much fun: few jumpscares and a lot of reading paperwork.

In her article, "A Reminder that Video Games Don't Have to Be Fun," Shonte Daniels says that expectations of enjoyment actually "stifle the gaming industry." She adds, "Once players acknowledge that games are about all human experiences, and not just the fun ones, then the games will only get better."

Daniels makes an important point here: If we insist on a game being "enjoyable," that excludes much of the human experience from being portrayed in games.

Depression, anxiety, and guilt aren't enjoyable. To draw out James's feelings of stress and loss and confusion, the designers chose to make the player stressed and lost and confused at the expense of fun.

The sound design by Akira Yamaoka had to be minimal. *Silent Hill* and its sequel share similar musical qualities, but the theme of the first game is jaunty and spooky. *Silent Hill 2*'s theme, a melancholic rock instrumental, feels more jarring and sad. Yet music throughout both games is relatively sparse—complementing the mood rather than setting it.

Yet there again lies the paradox of sequels. You make a sequel too similar, and you're criticized for cashing in on a hot property. You make a sequel too different, and you're losing what made people love it in the first place. *Silent Hill 2* stands somewhere between the two. As a visual experience, it's extremely similar to its predecessor, if obviously benefitting from newer, cooler technology. The character design, monster design, and aesthetic of the town tie the two games together.

But the original *Silent Hill* featured more action and excitement. The two share similar control schemes and progression systems, but from the moment a monster bursts through the window of the diner, *Silent Hill* feels fun. *Silent Hill 2*'s heavier focus on story and mood change how we approach it. Even calling the game "survival horror" feels misleading; we're rarely scared and even more rarely worried about surviving.

It's understandable some contemporary critics would find this disappointing.

Erik Wolpaw, who later went on to contribute amazing writing to the Portal series, gave a less than stellar review in *Computer Gaming World* in 2003 for the PC release of *Silent Hill 2*. He gives it only two stars, complaining, "*Silent Hill 2* doesn't make sense even when judged against the already lax sense-making standards of the survival horror genre." Wolpaw even ends his review focusing on how *not* enjoyable the game is. "With its lackadaisical pace, clumsy action sequences, and surreal atmosphere that's more disjointed than disturbing, *Silent Hill 2* is a nightmare, but only to play."

Ironically, what Wolpaw disliked about the game was itself the intention of its creators. In an interview with *OPM* in 2001, producer Akihiro Imamura said, "The fear of not being able to see what's ahead or around you is something that really disturbs human beings." The slow pace of the game and surreal atmosphere may detract from immediate gratification, but it adds to the player's *immersion* within the game.

Wolpaw's criticism that the game isn't conventionally scary is valid in context. Gamers were used to the jump scares and limited resources of games such as *Resident Evil* or even the first *Silent Hill*. That's part of what made them exciting. In *Silent Hill 2*, we don't even fight our first monster until a solid half hour into the game. Instead, we walk and we look, much like we do in modern walking simulators such as *What Remains of Edith Finch* or *Everybody's Gone to the Rapture*. What we learn about James and the other characters is *horrible* to be sure, but it's not what critics and fans may have been expecting.

The "fun" in the Grand Theft Auto games is found in doing whatever you want. The freedom is satisfying, even in failure. With Mario, the fun comes from discovery and the compelling game physics that make those discoveries possible. *Silent Hill 2*, however, builds an unhappy town populated by unhappy characters, denying the player any sense of fun. This choice may reduce the moment-to-moment enjoyment, but it makes the game more compelling as a whole.

As Andrei Nae writes in "Immersion at the Intersection of Technology, Subjectivity and Culture":

> Nonetheless, the small number of available movements, and the pre-scripted nature of the plot in *Silent Hill 2* and other video games ensure that the game entertains a high degree of playability and narrativity which then maintain a strong ludic and narrative engagement with the game. Were

this not the case, the game would become boring.

Controlling James is awkward because James himself is awkward. Limitations counterintuitively drive the narrative better than they would if James could steal a car or jump on enemies. There's little of the disconnect between a pre-planned story and gameplay that we see in games such as *Red Dead Redemption 2*. In a story about hard men trying to become better people, we're given the option to kill dozens of innocents on trains and in towns. It may make the game more exciting to play, but it flattens the theme of redemption.

Silent Hill 2 also refuses to hold its players' hands or break the fourth wall. There's no tutorial or introductory sequence to acclimate us to gameplay. As the game opens, we're left to our own devices on what to do in that gross bathroom. We never see a pop-up "Press B to Wash Face" moment that signals the interaction between controller, gamer, and avatar. Without fourth-wall–breaking intrusions, we are closer to James.

When James "wakes up" in the bathroom, the player can try to open doors, look at every urinal and mirror, and ultimately learn where to go—out. We need to figure out for ourselves what to do. From this perspective, the point of the bathroom is to leave the bathroom. Excepting, of course, the blue gem found in the bathroom after completing both the main game and "Born from a Wish." Considering that this blue gem is used to get the "UFO" ending, placing it near moldy toilets at the very beginning of the game feels like a joke from the developers.

Facing confusion until finding the "right door" establishes a gameplay precedent for the rest of the game. When you don't know what to do, James doesn't know what to do.

This extends to the map system. James enters a new area, James eventually finds an unmarked map of the area, and then James automatically "marks" the map as he progresses, noting which doors open and which doors are locked or blocked. It's exploration through pure trial and error.

Entering a room can cause battles that result in your death, which itself causes the worst possible fate: having to start over from an earlier save. *Silent Hill 2* encourages the player to just run down hallways, rapidly pressing the action button on every door, afraid to find one that does open.

Afraid being the operative word.

No matter how often I play *Silent Hill 2*, I don't want to run down those dark hallways. I get lost. I get frustrated. I scramble to avoid monsters. And. I. Click. On. Every. Door. It's not fun, but it is stressful. It's a system that fills you with dread. Even when you're not terrified in *Silent Hill 2*, you're anxious. It makes us feel the way James feels. The horror is less in the shock and more in the knowledge we *will* be shocked. Something bad is coming, we just know it.

Nor does this ever really change in the game. I love the Resident Evil series, but there's a point in almost every game where the tone switches from spooky survival horror to blowing shit up. Zombies are easier to face with a grenade launcher. Terrifying creatures soon become fun distractions.

But here, it's almost always in the player's best interest to simply run away. Not because the monsters are a threat, but because defeating them doesn't contribute any form of incentive outside of their removal from our immediate danger. There are no experience points, no skill tree, no loot to find.

James also gets tired. If you run too long, he breathes hard and needs a moment. He's human and he's just doing his best, man. He just saw a moaning flesh demon spray acid from its face; he needs a break. We literally can't run and gun this game because running makes normal people tired.

It adds a dimension to the character in a subtle, powerful way. To me, it almost feels like seeing a moment of weakness in a parent. Not because I thought of James as a father figure—no, my parents were way worse in different ways. Rather, it emphasizes human vulnerability.

It's also another reason why *Silent Hill 2* holds up. Games may have more advanced visuals, but the distance between the gameplay of single-player experiences in 2001 and the gameplay of single-player experiences now aren't that far apart. *Grand Theft Auto V* and *Red Dead Redemption 2* have almost the same tutorial beats that *Grand Theft Auto III* did. Games still largely feature power fantasies (as, it should be noted, do popular television shows and movies; it's not unique). *Silent Hill 2* still feels like a refreshing departure from the norm in its unpleasantness and refusal to give in to a more traditionally enjoyable gaming experience.

At the 2009 Montreal International Games Summit, *Waking Mars* designer Randy Smith said that it's important for games trying to evoke negative emotions to prevent the player from finding loopholes that would ease the experience. He describes a fictional game in which players are forced to deal with poverty and death while running a hospital. If you want the serious tone of the game to have weight, Smith argues, the experience of playing the game can't be too enjoyable. "If [the game] was like this, it would totally fail, because you'd have the player zipping around this depressing environment and winning because they figured it out."

James's weakness enhances our experience. His lack of traditional progress or empowerment narrows what we can do, eliminating distractions and deviations and narrative dissonance. The game works to rob us of "positive" gameplay loops the same way it works to rob us of "positive" narrative turns.

This may create an atmospheric, emotional experience for the player, but it also clearly created some trouble for Konami's advertising team.

There's a strange, scattered quality to the advertising that preceded the release of *Silent Hill 2*. I'm not saying it's unusual—video game ads of the era often pivoted away from the game itself to focus on style and attitude. Some of these campaigns were successful (e.g., "Genesis does what Nintendon't"), while some come off like the advertising company had no idea what a video game even is. Unfortunately, *Silent Hill 2's campaign* seems to be the latter.

Take for example one magazine ad.

The ad is a two-page spread with a bloody handprint on the left side. Blurred inside that handprint is a picture of James's face in red and black. Over that image, in an appropriately creepy font, are the words, "Wounds will heal…" On the right-hand page is a collage of characters' faces. Eddie, the chubby, bullied teen archetype, looks unintentionally comical, almost like a parody of a Chucky doll. On this page, the sentence finishes, "…but your mind will be scarred forever."

Almost as an afterthought, the ad features four small screenshots at the bottom right side of the page. Two of the shots are characters' faces from cutscenes, while the middle left features combat and the middle right has James looking down at a bloodied body. We also get the standard logo for the game, along with the ESRB rating. Believe it or not, *Silent Hill 2* got an M for Mature.

To use an academic term, this ad is lame as hell. Imagine if you were a customer and never heard of the Silent Hill series. The ad tells you nothing about the game. You can barely even tell what the game is about outside of the broad horror genre! Are you supposed to already know who all those people are? They aren't pre-existing characters. Outside of a tiny screenshot, a PlayStation logo, and an ESRB rating, you wouldn't even be certain it was a game at all.

Of course, ads for games have often valued stills and footage from slick pre-rendered cutscenes over gameplay. You might remember the ad campaign for *Final Fantasy VII* making it look like a Pixar film for grownup teens rather than a (delightful) game filled with chunky polygons.

Silent Hill 2's ads feel like the result of a room of writers at a whiteboard saying, "Boys! We need to sell this horror game! It's about a guy in a weird town looking for his dead wife! We got a dozen terrifying monsters, and a deep storyline about love and loss! But we can't use any of that! Let's get some ideas on the table!"

But they have my sympathy! For a sequel to a successful game, *Silent Hill 2* is remarkably hard to sell in a two-page spread or short TV spot. None of the original characters return. The storyline is completely different. There's likely only one, small gameplay screenshot at the bottom of the magazine ad because, let's be honest, there's not a lot of gameplay variety to show.

So how do you market dread?

The North American television commercial for *Silent Hill 2* does a marginally better job—but only because TV is a moving medium. It features clips of Mary's letter narration from the game, intercut with action scenes including Pyramid Head and a few other enemies. We also see some quick bits of cutscenes spliced together with "rough" film artifacts like the ones from the David Fincher movie *Se7en*.

Here's the weird part: This ad *opens* with James in a rowboat, which itself is from the "Rebirth" ending to the game. It's not really a spoiler—without playing the game, you'd have no idea what's actually happening. On the other hand, the "Rebirth" ending is relatively difficult to achieve, requiring multiple playthroughs and a fair amount of luck if you don't have a walkthrough. It's strange to open a video game commercial with a scene from the video game that the majority of players will never see.

The commercial seems to struggle for something interesting to show, so they use quick cuts to heighten tension in scenes that aren't that intense. Rather than a slow burn personal tragedy, *Silent Hill 2* looks like a bloody action game in which you gotta get your ass in there and save a beautiful woman. Blow some monsters away, kiss the girl, get home in time for Oprah.

To be fair, it would be far worse if ads and commercials gave away *Silent Hill 2*'s secrets. You can't ruin the surprise of the game! Ads for *The Sixth Sense* didn't say, "Bruce Willis has been dead the whole time." The twist is the whole point, right? Also, if you didn't know, Bruce Willis had been dead the whole time. Saved you two hours.

While the TV spot shows you *a little* of what you do in the game, the scenes move too fast. There's little sign of exploration, itself the vast majority of what we do in the game. You can't even really tell how the action works outside of enemies walking towards James, whom we're left to assume we play as.

One United Kingdom *Silent Hill 2* television ad is far worse—it doesn't even feature footage from the game. Instead, it revolves around a child hiding in a spooky forest and getting surprised by some random scary woman followed by a title card reading, "Better than your worst nightmare." From the box art at the end of the commercial, we know it's a video game, but nothing—genuinely nothing—in this ad reflects the actual experience of the game. There's no male child hiding from a witch in a forest. At least the American commercial showed a little gameplay. Here, the commercial can be reduced to someone saying "Boo!"

Another ad from the European Union suffers from a similar problem. On the bright side, this one at least does manage to incorporate *some* gameplay. However, it also mixes in dramatic black and white footage of a creepy corridor with little spooky phrases such as "no escape" and "infected flesh" appearing on the screen. The effect would've probably looked edgy in 2001. But again, there's not much information about the game itself. What the fuck is this game supposed to even *be*?

There is a fair argument to be made that you don't really have much info you can convey in under a minute. However, there's a huge disconnect between the slow, methodical game that is *Silent Hill 2* and these fast-cut ads that look like they could've been a Nine Inch Nails video.

Kirkland points out in "Discursively Constructing the Art of Silent Hill" that the ads do not focus on the game's puzzles. "The consequence is an emphasis on the games' narrative rather than ludic qualities, displaying more culturally prized cinematic artistry over less critically recognized video game aspects." In *The Terror Engine*, Perron agrees: "If there is one expression from Konami's own advertising that has been repeated throughout all of the games, it's probably the notion that Silent Hill delivers a 'cinematic horror experience.'" These are good points—to this day, movies are usually treated as more artistically significant than games. Konami emphasizes the watching more than the playing because they consider the playing less interesting.

On the flip side, none of these ads do anything to convey the sense of sadness and dread in that narrative that are driven by the gameplay experience. It's like taking the movie *Requiem for a Dream*, a depressing movie about drug abuse in New York, and making a trailer that only showed the parts where they were hanging out, having a good time, and then suddenly weeping. The ads privilege the *idea* of a narrative more than the actual damn narrative.

There's a spectacle to the ads that isn't quite present in the game. The ads are bigger and badder. They crib the aesthetics of contemporary movies in hopes the audience will connect to the game through something a little more in the consciousness of pop culture. Philip L. Simpson writes in in his essay, "The Horror "Event" Movie,"

> Through the deployment of spectacle made possible by technological advances in effects technology, paired with the traditional 'cliffhanger' narrative structure of escalation

of crisis, the horror event movie all but bludgeons the audience into a participatory interest in the onscreen proceedings.

It seems Konami's marketing team was taking this strategy for their commercials instead of connecting the game to the arthouse horror of David Lynch that inspired it. Show some pretty graphics, give a tense "cliffhanger" and "bludgeon" the audience with imagery until they're interested. In other words, they're trailers. But they also range from somewhat misleading to "kid who's not in the game hiding in a forest that's not in the game from a woman who's not in the game."

Konami's Japanese and E3 English-language trailers do a far better job, giving us longer scenes with inter-actions between characters and far more gameplay. We have a more coherent sense of story, hinting that Konami trusted Japanese and enthusiast gamers more than they did the unwashed masses. Fans and the press got a real taste of what Konami intended while regular audiences got every brand sold at Hot Topic thrown into a blender.

The E3 trailer does have a few major spoilers, although they're so scattered that it's hard to imagine anyone even realizing they're spoilers before playing the game. One weird moment, however, is the inclusion of the chain-saw weapon in an action scene. This, like the "Rebirth" ending, is only possible to get on a second playthrough of the game. It feels misleading here, like Konami wanted something *a little more badass*. "Yeah, yeah, sadness, guilt, you get. But also—a CHAINSAW!"

Sony's 2001 E3 press conference is also worth a watch, if only because of how outrageously awkward those things used to be. Oh, you think gaming press conferences are weird now with their massive budgets and B-list celebrities reading off a teleprompter? Buckle up, because E3 events used to be masterclasses in the art of making us all feel ashamed for liking video games.

Here's the good news: Sony actually ends their 2001 press conference with both *Silent Hill 2* and *Metal Gear Solid 2*. It's now so easy to forget just how important Konami was to the PlayStation brand in its first decade. To steal from another company's ad campaign, Metal Gear Solid and Silent Hill were examples of what Sony did that Nintendidn't.

Here's the bad news: *Silent Hill 2* was *clearly* less important than *Metal Gear Solid 2*. The first *Silent Hill* was a success, but *Metal Gear Solid* was a phenomenon. While discussing the new games, the Sony representative heaps (well-deserved!) praise on Hideo Kojima while rushing through his introduction of *Silent Hill 2* executive producer Gozo Kitao.

Kitao gives a brief introduction in English, and then switches to Japanese with a live translator. With his blazer and measured delivery, Kitao comes off more as a business manager than a rock star like Kojima.

Still, Kitao hits an important point early on when he talks about the lessons his team took from the original game: "We analyzed why we got so much attention, and we realized that is attributed to the special psychological horror, or chilling feeling that you cannot experience with any other programs."

Kitao expands on this, talking about the then-recently released PlayStation 2. He says they saw the PlayStation 2's power as a way to "create peculiar feelings of this atmosphere of horror." To Kitao, the new technological power is the key to the "unique horror that you can only feel through the games—that you cannot achieve through watching movies or TV programs."

What's so fascinating about this press conference to me is the vast gulf between the ads and the developers. The print and television ads almost completely fail to convey any of the psychological horror of the game, while Kitao is straight up just *explaining it*. Kitao emphasizes the idea that a horror game can provide a superior experience to traditional media.

Kitao finally introduces Imamura and Sato to show off the game itself. Remember when I said that Kitao was clearly a businessman? Well, Imamura and Sato are clearly creatives—both dress and speak more casually than Kitao.

Here, again, we have a departure from the ads: Imamura shows off gameplay! And not just action, either—straight up "reading letters on a desk" gameplay while he talks about the "atmosphere" of the town. Curiously, the gameplay footage appears to largely *avoid* combat—on screen, James runs past monsters and enters different rooms, with only one or two brief encounters. Imamura thereby signals to viewers that the game is not *about* combat. Also worth noting is that there aren't any jump scare moments in the entire presentation. That and the clear emphasis on atmosphere really drive home the idea this is a psychological game, not a zombie shoot 'em up.

Like Kitao, Imamura is also extremely focused on the technical aspects of the game's horror—the fog and the narrow bands of light make it so that gameplay proceeds "with the fear that something, someone, is hiding in the dark." Spooky *and* accurate!

After Imamura's technical demo and explanation of the game, Sato steps up. Sato, with his leather jacket and dyed hair is the most Kojima of the bunch.

Notable in Sato's segment is his mention of a "romantic" story that requires high-quality CGI for "drama." Calling it "romantic" is a clever choice. After all, James is on a traditionally romantic quest: saving a loved one. We just don't yet know that he also killed that loved one.

Sato takes time to explain the work that went into the character design and cutscenes. He's clearly proud of the way the pre-rendered full motion video flows seamlessly into the gameplay, another quality later ruined by the HD update of the games, as we'll soon discuss.

There's a contagious glee to this side of the presentation. While some of Sato's English-language jokes don't land (the audience seems particularly confused by a line where he says developing the game saved "fat on my belly"), you can't help but smile at how much he loves this masterpiece.

The presentation ends with Kitao coming back out, re-explaining that the demo reel is a bit out of date, and then saying he hopes the game would be released in the fall of 2001, which it was.

If you're not a fan of technical details, much of this presentation can be boring. But this presentation also *understands the game* in a way that conventional ads and commercials clearly didn't. It may seem odd to so specifically lay out the technical details of fog and sound effects, but it's successful at delivering the message that they're trying to make something different than other horror games. Not once do they refer to the competition specifically, but you can tell how much they want *Silent Hill 2* to stand out as a unique title.

It's a shame that this excitement displayed by Kitao and friends gets lost in the marketing of the game. While Kirkland and Perron say that the choice to focus on CGI clips and story beats over gameplay means Konami itself wanted to connect *Silent Hill 2* to cinematic experiences, I'm not sure it's entirely that simple. "Konami the company" and "Konami the team of developers behind *Silent Hill 2*" are, after all, not one entity. While it may be a business conference, Konami's presentation at E3 is still intended to *sell* the game. There's just a gulf between how the game's producers sell it and how the corporate ads sell it. Both are talking to different audiences, but both also reveal a different perspective on which aspects of the game matter to the consumer.

Nor is this just academic. Marketing affects the expectations of both the public and the games press. While *Silent Hill 2* did well upon release with sales going into the hundreds of thousands even before the Xbox version was released, reviewers largely seemed annoyed by the change of pace from the original. According to Metacritic, *Silent Hill 2* (on the PS2) is the 47th best rated game of 2001, ranking just below upcoming Boss Fight Books subject, *NASCAR Racing 4*. Now, that's still an aggregate score of 89. Not bad! But 47th place is rough if we're only looking at a single year's output of games.

Game Informer was especially displeased. In a review titled, "Big Fogging Disappointment," Justin Leeper says, "Instead of the brain-bending adventure with scares and gore that I had so desperately hoped for, it turned out to be a sloppy, monotonous bore that nearly put me to sleep."

Silent Hill 2 is less scary and less gory than the original. The story itself is smaller and sadder. There's no giant cult murdering children to raise a demonic god. There's just a guy who's bummed about the crappy thing he did. In retrospect, that's specifically what makes *Silent Hill 2* such a great game. But at the time, it felt like a dramatic step back to many people.

This disappointment shouldn't be surprising. If *Aliens* was the action-packed sequel to the subtle, slow *Alien*, then *Silent Hill 2* is the subtle, slow sequel to the action-packed *Silent Hill*. Just because you loved one doesn't mean you'll love the other.

Joe Fielder of GameSpot was similarly let down by the game, saying,

Hopes have been high that the game's PlayStation 2 sequel would provide a more satisfying storyline on top of the graphical improvements expected from the series' jump onto a next-generation game system. It succeeds in that, in a sense, but loses some of the original game's appeal along the way. […] *Silent Hill 2* is a much prettier, somewhat smarter but less-compelling game than the original.

Translation: "Really good graphics, but kinda boring." I'm being unfair. Fielder did give the game 7.7—respectable, but not fantastic. However, almost every one of Fielder's criticisms are more or less preferences for the original rather than a problem with the sequel itself:

Silent Hill 2 is creepier than the first game, but it's not scarier. For example, one of the monsters in the original was a half dog/half man that chased you through the mist and let out a gruff bark capable of making the hair on the back of your neck stand up. *Silent Hill 2*'s creatures may look as disturbing, but you tend to destroy them because they're in your way and you're carrying a lot of ammunition, not because you're afraid or fighting for your life.

Even as IGN appreciated the "unstable, untrustworthy characters, incredible atmosphere, and [the] slow, creepy haunt of a story," it couldn't quite square the palpable emotional impact with disappointment in gameplay:

Still, the game doesn't break any molds or revolutionize the survival-horror genre in any particular way, but it tells a hard to figure, surreal story that's strangely heartbreaking and even a tad depressing.

It's very curious, though, how IGN's Aaron Boulding briefly touches on one of *Silent Hill 2*'s best elements: its exploration.

You end up doing a lot of running through the buildings and streets of Silent Hill. In fact, you do more running than anything. […] But the running around is how you experience the game's most important element: the creepiness. You're running around dark and dingy hallways through thick layers of fog that seems to cling to the ground. It's when you're shuttling back and forth that you'll hear all of the scary sounds of creatures far off in the distance. And this is when you realize that you're not just running in circles for no good reason. *Silent Hill 2* relentlessly messes with your sense of well-being.

There we go!

While most reviews, including the above, complain about the lack of straightforward action (and conflate scariness with difficult combat), Boulding touches on an important point about *Silent Hill 2*. The exploration doesn't serve the narrative. The exploration *is* the narrative. The gameplay isn't fun candy between cutscenes, it's a foundation that makes those cutscenes matter.

Silent Hill 2 felt so unique that even its own company wasn't entirely sure how to sell it. For many critics, the game's greatest strengths—story, atmosphere, exploration—often counted against it. Beset by players who expected a bigger, badder sequel and corporate ads that painted the game as a gothic gore fest, only the developers of *Silent Hill 2* knew they were creating something truly unique.

Although I have to be honest, "Big Fogging Disappointment" is a great review title.

YOU CAN'T REMASTER
HOME AGAIN

THE FIRST VIDEO GAME REMASTER I can remember truly being excited about was *Super Mario All-Stars*. I was a tiny, annoying child who liked Super Mario. I still am. The idea of the same games being available with *better graphics in one cartridge* was the dream. When kids around the cafeteria would talk about desert island games, I thought I had the perfect loophole: Four whole games at once! I was a child genius.

But game remakes and remasters are a weird beast. Movies have always treated "remakes" with wild abandon: Take the core conceit of the original and go wild with it. Maybe add in the tiniest bit of connective tissue to link the plot to the original and call it a "reboot." Done; insert cash register sound.

Then there's the movie "remaster"—a touching up of the print, maybe "restoring" a scene that the director loved. Cleared up picture, sound, and color—usually released on a newer, higher-definition format. These tend to be extremely reverent to the source material. The goal isn't to change, but to preserve.

Video games, however, are more complicated than films. Movies usually look better in 4K than they did on an old CRT television. Older games, however, lose their clarity. Pixels become chunky. Textures blur. Even professional re-releases can be prone to problems. The NES and Nintendo 64 emulators on the Wii U were famously dark and muddy. If you were experiencing *Paper Mario* for the first time, you'd think the entire game took place during a somewhat cloudy day. It's cheaper to rush an emulation than it is to take the time and team effort to make that original game shine on modern monitors.

Of course, there is hope. Nintendo's emulation has gotten generally better on the Switch—although they could have fixed the goddamn camera in *Super Mario 64*. Meanwhile, publishers like Capcom and SNK have worked with developers such as Digital Eclipse on compilations that try as hard as they can to replicate the feel and look of the original—often even including box art and manuals, themselves an underrated part of the experience.

Unfortunately, some video game remasters often end up in the "Star Wars Special Edition" category. You know what I mean. The Star Wars Special Editions that added bad CG and weird story changes. The same goes for the *E.T.* 20th anniversary edition that replaced guns with walkie talkies. They're the movies that didn't need fixing but get "fixed" until they're broken.

Unlike movies, old games are annoyingly difficult to play on today's platforms without some dedication and/or shadiness. If you own a DVD copy of a movie from 2001, it'll work on any current console with a disc drive. Pop it in, and you can watch. It might not be the highest quality available, but it works! A game from 2001, however, either requires setting up an emulator or using unofficial HDMI conversion devices. These methods are effective, but they're not intuitive for the casual gamer.

Accessing old games isn't always the problem—actually finding a way to play them is. This creates a great market for old and new fans who want to play the classics without the hassle of illegal ROMs, complicated mods, or long-dead hardware.

So do you emulate a game as closely as possible to the original experience or remaster it so it "looks" and "sounds" better for a modern audience with modern expectations?

This problem isn't unique to games and movies. Music has long been a battleground for purists, especially with the resurgence of vinyl bringing back that sweet analog sound. Any art form will look, feel, and sound different than it did with earlier technology.

Video games, however, carry a unique challenge: the past.

With games, emulated remakes and remasters tend to rely on nostalgia, making it impossible to create a perfect experience for fans who haven't played on an old cathode ray tube TV in years. The choices help, but they often muddy what should be a "pure" experience. Scanlines—a recreation of the look of older televisions—can feel artificial. Meanwhile, the pixel art aesthetic may seem the closest to the original, but its chunky style and sharp corners are also not how the games originally looked.

Meanwhile, full-on remakes can lose or change some of the "feel" of the original. The *Resident Evil* remake for GameCube is rightfully beloved for being beautiful and gothic, yet it loses much of the fun cheese of the original. The original *Resident Evil* felt like an independent horror movie from the 70s. Its remake feels more like a modern horror film, grittier and darker and somewhat self-aware. Both work! But they're certainly not the same game.

And so we come to *Silent Hill HD Collection*. Not a remake, but barely a remaster—more a breaking of the game by polishing away everything that made it work.

Silent Hill HD Collection tries to have it both ways and fails both ways. Released for the PS3 and Xbox 360, *Silent Hill HD Collection* was intended to just bring two games from the series onto modern consoles with clearer graphics and updated voices.

On one hand, they succeeded in that mission. On the other hand, that success ruins *Silent Hill 2*.

Right off the bat, the fact that the package is called *Silent Hill HD Collection* and doesn't include the first *Silent Hill* is an atrocity. While *Silent Hill 2* works perfectly fine as a standalone game, *Silent Hill 3* ultimately makes less sense unless you've played the original. Why would they leave that out? Probably so they could sell more copies of the original *Silent Hill* for PS3 (and PSP/Vita) in Sony's online store.

Not including the foundation of the series is frustrating, but it's not the reason this collection is so hated. The high definition graphical improvements touted by the title turned out just to be a higher resolution and widened aspect ratio, neither of which actually improve the experience. According to Richard Leadbetter's Eurogamer article, "What Went Wrong with Silent Hill HD?", Hijinks, the company responsible for the re-release, basically took the assets from the PlayStation 2 version and made them work on 16:9 televisions. "Aside from typography and UI elements, there is very little evidence that there has actually been any kind of actual 'remastering' of original artwork at all."

How do you remaster *Silent Hill 2*, one of the best-looking games on the PS2, and make it look worse? *Silent Hill 2* is a beautiful game. Sure, some background architecture looks unimpressive by today's standards, but Sato's character design remains iconic. Having patched the PC version of the game to work on a modern computer, there's honestly no excuse for *Silent Hill 2* ever looking bad. If dedicated fans can make the game stay beautiful on newer screens, Konami could have too.

The removal of fog effects "clears up" the graphics, but reveals many of the rough edges that were never intended to be seen by players. Fog helped ease graphical processing on the PS2 and was also one of the most important factors in the game's atmosphere. With fog, Silent Hill is a town of mystery, horror, and the unknown. As Angela says early in the game, the fog is specifically *why* it's hard to find your way around town. It also adds a sense of romance and dreaminess, as if James could be hallucinating everything. Fog even ties together the game's motif of water and breathing.

The difference between the original and *HD Collection* is like the one between a set as it looks in a movie and in behind-the-scenes footage. In the movie, the set looks and feels real. You don't see the edges where craft services wait with bagels. In behind-the-scenes footage, you can see the slick of paint on the wall, expensive props now clearly made of plastic. The same applies here.

Let's try another example. You know when you come home for the holidays and your boomer parents' television has that terrible motion smoothing that makes hundred-million-dollar movies look like an old British Christmas special? It's like that. It's not unwatchable, but the whole experience feels wrong.

The same problem plagues cutscenes in the game using pre-rendered video. *Silent Hill 2*'s cutscenes were rendered to fit the resolution and aspect ratio of most televisions in 2001. As Eurogamer notes, no effort was made to re-render or bump up the resolution of these cutscenes. Instead, the videos feel fuzzy and overtly old. Without seamless transitions into these scenes, *HD Collection* inserts a wedge between narrative and gameplay.

It's worth returning to the Star Wars Special Edition comparison here. George Lucas added all these special effects that somehow both looked out of place *and* made the older special effects look worse. That's how the cutscenes in *HD Collection* appear without having been re-rendered or adjusted. They don't fit at all, and it feels like watching an old low-res YouTube video rather than experiencing the game's dramatic, immediate moments.

These aren't minor quibbles from a fan. The graphical details really do make or break the experience. A foggy graveyard, a misty city street—those locations create tension. You don't know what's coming and you don't know where you're going. It isolates the player and keeps their attention focused. Being able to see the "seams" of the game flattens all that.

Then there's issue of the new voice acting. Fans were so upset when Konami announced the new voices that Konami created the option for players to use the original VO if they wanted. Monica Horgan's Mary/Maria, Guy Cihi's James, Donna Burke's Angela, David Schaufele's Eddie, and Jackie (misspelled in the game's credits as "Jakey") Breckenridge's Laura are vital pieces of the experience. All of them absolutely nail the game's air of confusion and despair.

Much like the removal of fog and other effects, the change in voice acting came down to a well-meaning technical "upgrade" to 5.1 surround sound audio. In an interview on GameFront, producer Tom Hulett (who also worked as a producer on the Silent Hill games *Origins*, *Downpour*, and more) defended the decision to get new voices:

> So we have new voices because we wanted to do a 5.1 audio mix, since it's HD. The old voices are all stereo, so we can't just re-use the old voice files. So we re-recorded all the voices, but at the same time, wanting to provide the perfect experience for fans, we pursued getting the rights to use the original voices for a stereo mix if fans wanted it.

Getting rights to the original voices is admirable! And going for 5.1 meshes with Konami's business interests.

If you're a company in 2012 making a high-definition remaster of classic games, you want that 5.1 audio mix feature on the box. As they say on *House Hunters*, it adds "curb appeal."

Except, just like the fog, the graininess and loose quality of the dialogue *is* the game. Assuming that crisp, exact sound would improve the *Silent Hill 2* experience misses the point of it entirely. What we end up getting doesn't sound like remastered audio, but an odd, new dubbing that doesn't quite work. It's a little too clean, a little too polished.

Yet it also doesn't sound like Hijinx was given much of a choice. As Hulett explained in a Reddit AMA, "management said we would be rerecording the original voices, so I volunteered to handle it. At the time I was not assigned to the project at all (busy with [*Silent Hill: Book of Memories*]). With my background from Atlus and track record with VO I thought I could ensure that a drastic change would be handled as appropriately as possible."

Hulett was the front-facing person on the project, but he didn't deserve a lot of the fan backlash he received. That blame more likely rests on Konami, a company who has shown an incredible knack for not understanding their own games. Only a few years later, they'd cancel *Silent Hills*, whose demo *P.T.* is the second-best game in the entire series. It's easy to imagine Konami demanding quick and easy "upgrades" to the games they could advertise.

In fairness, new voices aren't even that bad. Troy Baker is an amazing video game voice actor, but his James is too gruff and masculine. He sounds too much like a depressed version of a standard video game hero, whereas Guy Cihi's James is beautifully lost. This also applies to Angela, whose new voice by veteran voice actor Laura Bailey sounds just a bit more like a helpful anime character than Donna Burke's ageless suicidal woman dealing with trauma. There's just an added hamminess for most of the characters—with the exception of Maria, who's inexplicably been tuned down a bit emotionally. None of it is quite right.

Would my experience be different if I had never played the original *Silent Hill 2*? Sure! Anything is possible with the power of imagination! But that's like saying I would like Nicolas Cage screaming about the bees in *The Wicker Man* (2006) if I hadn't seen the 1973 original. Maybe, but the original *does* exist, so we *can* judge a remaster by it.

Remember the found footage fad in horror movies? The graininess and shakiness of the camera added an unreal quality that we all found captivating after years of smooth, overproduced films that looked and sounded a bit too good for us to suspend our disbelief.

The original versions' misty visuals and distant, estranged voice acting intentionally create the same effect. As Imamura put it in his OPM interview, "In *Silent Hill 2*, we are really proud of the analog film kind of style. We wanted to create as non-polygonal-ish an image as possible. That's why the game has the noisy look to it." It's like *The Blair Witch Project*. The conceit of hapless friends recording each other as they experience trauma has been used and reused so many times since then, it's now a cliché. But it's a cliché for a reason. The analogue quality of video tape static *feels* more real because it's older and forgotten.

Now imagine if that footage in *The Blair Witch Project* was completely cleaned up, given better camera angles, more lighting, and an HD sheen. Suddenly, the woods just look like woods and the terrified friends appear to be the actors they are.

That's the difference.

Whether intended or not, that meta-experience is powerful, and *Silent Hill HD Collection* takes it away by trying to smooth out those edges. This only highlights how tiny details in the original game add up to create such a compelling journey. *Silent Hill 2* doesn't work despite its quirks—it works *because* of its quirks.

Pull one Jenga block from *Silent Hill 2* and the rest of the experience falls apart. Without the right acting, it becomes melodramatic and corny. Without the right aesthetics, the town becomes a generic video game setting. Much like many of its inspirations, the Silent Hill series relies on the uncanny to unnerve the player.

Attempts to spruce it up in remakes or project contemporary horror movie tropes in ads don't do the game justice—they just make an incredible experience a bit more average. James and Mary's story requires a tone and aesthetic that evokes emotional loss and darkness; the town needs to feel both familiar and absolutely confounding; the gameplay has to derive players of power rather than feed into the fantasy. This is what shocks us. This is what scares us. This is what makes trying to open doors in a hospital so stress-inducing.

The Silent Hill series may have started as an attempt to ride the 90s survival horror craze, but—at least for a while—it found something deeper than zombies and dogs jumping through windows. In an artform filled with epic tales of ancient evils endangering the future of the world, *Silent Hill 2* focused on something more human, a story with tragic characters in an eerily familiar setting that we find ourselves horrified to identify with. Through incredible character work, technological tricks, a dedicated team, and pure luck, Konami created a gut-wrenching masterpiece.

True, *Silent Hill 2* doesn't have something for everyone. It's antithetical to the average video game experience. It's not really fun in any traditional sense and it absolutely buries some of its most interesting gameplay dynamics. Even the hero of the game turns out to be not much of a hero at all, his quest ultimately one about repentance more than rescue. In this way, *Silent Hill 2* calls forward to many modern, narrative-heavy games in which winning is less important than experiencing. And as in the best stories, reaching the end of *Silent Hill 2* only creates more questions.

While rumors persist that a remake or a new Silent Hill game will appear on the new generation of consoles, and Pyramid Head now appears as a playable character in the action-horror game *Dead by Daylight*, none of what we've recently seen from the franchise comes close to James's walk into that mist-covered vacation town. It's a shame that the series is now best known for its enemy designs and rusted, bloody environments when the series is about so much more than that. Konami can sell shirts with *Silent Hill 2* characters on it, but they can't recreate the magic of the game that spawned them.

James probably shouldn't have murdered his wife, though.

NOTES

What Is Silent Hill 2?

Ewan Kirkland's article "Restless Dreams and Shattered Memories: Psychoanalysis and Silent Hill" was published in *Brumal: Research Journal on the Fantastic* vol. 3, issue 1 (2015): https://bit.ly/2ILscr0.

The Survival Horror Bandwagon

Official U.S. PlayStation Magazine's interview with Keiichiro Toyama and Takayoshi Sato was originally published in vol. 2, no. 6 (March 1999). The fan site Silent Hill Memories hosts a transcription of the interview: https://bit.ly/2KlPwMd.

Ewan Kirkland's "Masculinity in Video Games: The Gendered Gameplay of *Silent Hill*" was published in *Camera Obscura* vol. 24, no. 2 (September 2009): https://bit.ly/3lIFfrg.

Weekly Famitsu's 34/40 score for *Silent Hill* was awarded in issue 534 (vol. 14, no. 11), released March 12, 1999.

IGN's Francesca Reyes reviewed *Silent Hill* on February 24, 1999: https://bit.ly/2IUPKsU.

GameSpot's Joe Fielder reviewed *Silent Hill* on February 23, 1999: https://bit.ly/2IT38hg.

Game sales for *Silent Hill* are recorded at VGChartz: https://bit.ly/3pK4ax8.

IGN's interview with *Silent Hill 2* producer Akihiro Imamura was posted March 28, 2001, as "IGN PS2 Interviews Silent Hill 2 Producer Akihiro Imamura": https://bit.ly/38ZEdDG.

PlayStation Magazine's interview with Keiichiro Toyama was originally published in issue 19 (March 1999). Silent Hill Memories hosts a transcription of the interview: https://bit.ly/3fn7edJ.

The Akira Yamaoka quote and Akihiro Imamura citing the influence of David Lynch and *Twin Peak*s are each recorded in Bernard Perron's book *Silent Hill: The Terror Engine* (University of Michigan Press, 2012).

Takayoshi Sato notes his artistic influences in his interview with IGN's Douglass C. Perry, first published in August 2001: https://bit.ly/333cH4r.

Francis Bacon's "snail" quote is recorded at the Francis Bacon MB Art Foundation's "On His Art" quotations page: https://bit.ly/3nK4dHd.

Kevin F. Steinmetz's "Carceral Horror: Punishment and Control in *Silent Hill*" was published in *Crime, Media, Culture* vol. 14, issue 2 (2018): https://bit.ly/3fiiS9N.

A Peculiar Little Town

Harry S. Truman's quote from *Twin Peaks* comes from episode 3, "Zen, or the Skill to Catch a Killer."

Stephen King discusses the "Peculiar Little Towns" in his short story collection, *Nightmares & Dreamscapes*, 1993.

Inger Ekman and Petri Lankoski's "Hair-Raising Entertainment: Emotions, Sound, and Structure in *Silent Hill 2* and *Fatal Frame*" was published in *Horror Video Games: Essays on the Fusion of Fear and Play*, edited by Bernard Perron (McFarland & Co., 2009).

The script of "The Making of Silent Hill 2" is hosted at Silent Hill Memories: https://bit.ly/3pVdxKy. The documentary itself was filmed by Fun TV and released on a bonus DVD disc bundled with the European edition of *Silent Hill 2*.

Silent Hill Memories's "Trivia" page documents some real-world locations used in *Silent Hill 2*: https://bit.ly/36QFuKF.

Kirk Hamilton's November 1, 2012 Kotaku article "Woah, I Didn't Know *Kindergarten Cop* Took Place in Silent Hill" explores the visual connections of the first *Silent Hill* and the Schwarzenegger film: https://bit.ly/2UL16Tg.

Duncan Fyfe's "Survival Horror" was published at the Campo Santo Quarterly Review on October 10, 2015: https://bit.ly/32WnsFN. Leigh Alexander's quote also comes from here.

Your Villain, James Sunderland

Andrei Nae's "Immersion at the Intersection of Technology, Subjectivity and Culture: An Analysis of *Silent Hill 2*" was published in *Acta Universitatis Sapientiae, Film and Media Studies* vol.13, issue 1 (June 4, 2014): https://bit.ly/38ZIXcs.

Roberto Grosso's "Character Select: James Sunderland" was published at TechRaptor on May 20, 2016: https://bit.ly/2UInegP.

How Do You Solve a Problem Like Maria?

Jonathan Barkan's editorial "'Born from a Wish': Revisiting 'Silent Hill 2's' Extra Chapter" was published at Bloody Disgusting on October 10, 2016: https://bit.ly/35KwYNS.

Angela Did Nothing Wrong

Tarrah Rivard's "Character Spotlight – Angela Orosco" was published at Rely on Horror on August 17, 2011: https://bit.ly/2IRvJUA.

Ewan Kirkland's "Gothic Videogames, Survival Horror, and the *Silent Hill* Series" was published in *Gothic Studies* vol. 14, issue 2 (October 2018): https://bit.ly/35MIXKX.

Sarah E. Ullman, Liana C. Peter-Hagene, and Mark Relyea's "Coping, Emotion Regulation, and Self-Blame as Mediators of Sexual Abuse and Psychological Symptoms in Adult Sexual Assault" was published in the *Journal of Child Sexual Abuse* vol. 23, no. 1 (January 2014): https://bit.ly/2HmpJT8.

Fatty Falls Down

The study which describes the "bully-victim" is Clayton R. Cook, Kirk R. William, Nancy G. Guerra, Tia E. Kim, and Shelly Sadek's "Predictors of Bullying and Victimization in Childhood and Adolescence: A Meta-analytic Investigation," published in *School Psychology Quarterly* vol. 25, no. 2 (2010): https://bit.ly/2IWdDAh. The American Psychological Association reported the results of this study in July 2010 as "Who Is Likely to Become a Bully, Victim or Both?": https://bit.ly/3fJWkFM.

Alex Biedenbach's "Character Study: Eddie Dombrowski (Silent Hill 2)" was published at the blog Of A Sound Mind and Body: Thoughts on Disability in American Media on April 23, 2017: https://bit.ly/3lPCTqv.

Does Pyramid Head Matter?

Rémy Bennett's "Horror Films And Feminism: Women Who Don't Run From Danger, But Step Up To It (Thank You, Mary Shelley)" was published at Bust on November 16, 2015: https://bit.ly/3pVkmMa.

RagnarRox's "Pyramid Head." was uploaded to YouTube on May 9, 2015: https://youtu.be/BnvyKHMBipc?t=357.

No Happy Endings

Alexander Kriss's "Silent Hill 2's Endings Aren't What You Want, But What You Deserve" was published at Kill Screen on October 31, 2014: https://bit.ly/2UIpogr.

Sercan Şengün's "Silent Hill 2 and the Curious Case of Invisible Agency" was presented at the International Conference on Interactive Digital Storytelling 2013 and published in the conference proceedings *Interactive Storytelling* edited by Hartmut Koenitz et al. (Springer, 2013). A preprint copy is available at the author's website: https://bit.ly/2IVRtP3.

Ewan Kirkland's quote comes from "Discursively Constructing the Art of Silent Hill," published in *Games and Culture* vol. 5, issue 3 (2010): https://bit.ly/35NY5rv.

The novelization of *Silent Hill 2* is Sadamu Yamashita's *Sairento Hiru 2*, published in Japanese by Konami in 2006. An unofficial English translation of the novel is available at Ducky's English Translations: https://bit.ly/2ITsY51.

Playing and Selling Dread

Shonte Daniels's "A Reminder that Video Games Don't Have to Be Fun" was published at Vice Motherboard on May 19, 2015: https://bit.ly/3kNL59J.

Erik Wolpaw's review of Silent Hill 2's PC release, "Silent Hill 2: No Thrills and Maybe Two Chills" was published in *Computer Gaming World* issue 225 (April 2003). A copy is accessible via the Internet Archive: https://bit.ly/3pEWVqh.

Akihiro Imamura's interview with *Official U.S. PlayStation Magazine* (*OPM*) was originally published in the October 2001 issue as "Fear Factor." A transcript is available at the fan site Letter from Silent Heaven: https://bit.ly/3316B4N.

Chris Remo reported on Randy Smith's thoughts on games' enjoyability in "Randy Smith: Do Games Need To Be Fun?" published at Gamasutra on November 17, 2009: https://bit.ly/3347cCK.

The two-page "bloody handprint" spread can be seen at Whitney C.'s SilentHillCollection.com: https://bit.ly/3pNyHdh.

The North American television commercial for *Silent Hill 2* was uploaded on August 6, 2016 to Town of Silent Hill's YouTube channel as "Silent Hill 2: North American Commercial": https://youtu.be/upE9VnfA46A. The United Kingdom *Silent Hill 2* commercial was uploaded on April 19, 2009 to Silent Hill Memories's YouTube channel as "Silent Hill 2 UK TV Spot 45 (PS2)": https://youtu.be/PqolCH8i8Jg. The European Union commercial was uploaded on February 1, 2015 to PS2museum's YouTube channel as "Silent Hill 2 | PS2 | TV commercial EU 2001": https://youtu.be/a9fSrOJ7S-w.

Philip L. Simpson's chapter "The Horror 'Event' Movie: *The Mummy*, *Hannibal*, and *Signs*" was published in *Horror Film: Creating and Marketing Fear*, edited by Steffen Hantke (University Press of Mississippi, 2004).

Konami's presentation from the E3 2011 was uploaded to YouTube on July 28, 2014 by GrantBitman as "Silent Hill 2 - E3 2001 - Presentation by Konami": https://youtu.be/8QYqWQqEAdA.

Metacritic's ranking of the "Best Video Games for 2001" is here: https://bit.ly/3pMqfLm.

The *Game Informer* review "Big Fogging Disappointment" (with a URL dated October 2001 and signed by "Justin") is available at the Internet Archive: https://bit.ly/2HlHRwo. "Justin" is most likely Justin Leeper, whose blog Justin's This Just In identifies him as a former *Game Informer* journalist: https://bit.ly/35Msp5O.

Joe Fielder's review of *Silent Hill 2* was published at GameSpot on September 24, 2001: https://bit.ly/2IOYUau.

Ivan Sulic of IGN's review was published December 3, 2002: https://bit.ly/3m0e776.

You Can't Remaster Home Again

Richard Leadbetter's Eurogamer article, "What Went Wrong with Silent Hill HD?" was published on April 10, 2012: https://bit.ly/3nEtqmp.

Tom Hulett's interview with GameFront was published on January 4, 2012. Silent Hill Memories hosts a transcript: https://bit.ly/35MSqBV. Similarly, the site also hosts a transcript from Hulett's August 16, 2018 Reddit AMA: https://bit.ly/36RoHXN. The AMA is also threaded at the Silent Hill Community forums: https://bit.ly/3nDVczA.

ACKNOWLEDGEMENTS

To sum up, in conclusion, *Silent Hill 2* is a land of contrasts.

No, I'm sorry.

Let me start this one over.

For reasons that are both my fault and also my fault, this book took far longer than it should've to finish. It's not a very long book, either, so I've got no excuse. Fortunately, Gabe Durham was nice enough to give me all the time I needed, and then more time, and then even more time. Both Alyse Knorr and Mike Williams gave invaluable input and edits, while proofreaders Nick Sweeney, Joe M. Owens, Meghan Burklund, and Matthew LeHew helped keep me from sounding like the full idiot I am. Chris Moyer did incredible work on layout, as did Cory Schmitz on cover design.

Thank you to the friends who gave advice on writing the book, the other friends who read drafts of this book, and the family who are vaguely aware that I'm writing this book.

None of this book would have been possible without the Silent Hill fan community. Fans of this series do it all. They create mods to make *Silent Hill 2* playable in 2020. They transcribe and post ancient interviews from long-dead gaming magazines. They write intricate walkthroughs so I could know how to get that goddamn "Dog"ending. All that just scratches the surface. I can't be thankful enough of the many, many communities, ranging from r/SilentHill to Silent Hill Memories to the Silent Hill wiki to AlchemillaHospital.net. Any mistakes or omissions I've made in this book are entirely my own, not the good people who've kept the series alive.

Finally, thanks to the *Silent Hill 2* development team for creating one of the greatest games of all time. You really made me feel bad. Not the highest bar, but still good for a game.

SPECIAL THANKS

For making our fifth season of books possible, Boss Fight Books would like to thank John Romero, Ian Chung, Fenric Cayne, Trey Adams, Jennifer Durham-Fowler, Cathy Durham & Ed Locke, Ken Durham & Nancy Magnusson Durham, Nate Mitchell, Lawliet Tamaki Aivazis, Cassandra Newman, seanz0r, Zach Davis, Andrew "Xestrix" Carlson, Ant'ny Fataski, David Goodenough, Adam Hejmowski, Joshua Mallory, and Sean 'Ariamaki' Riedinger. Adam Rosenfield, Sileem Farghaly, Samuel Rauhala, mceaton, Nathan Tolf, brazzell dazzell, Todd Hansberger, Michael O'Leary, Connor Wack, Wes Locher, Yoan Sebdoun-Manny, Scott Mendenko, Jeff H, John Simms, Matthew LeHew, Aaron Murray, Jason 'XenoPhage' Frisvold, Kevin Foss, Mickey Possingham, Chris Suellentrop, Tim Suter, Yannick Rochat, Salvatore Pane, Anonymous, Josh Scherping, Joseph De Maria, J. Kyle Pittman, Bear Belcastro, Stephen Trinh, Shane Culp, Marc Beavan, Nik Zeltzer, Graham Guletz, Jonathan Charles Bruce, Samuel Kossow, Chris Furniss, Morgie73, David Altman, Dave Kapell, Justin "Vextalon" Brissette,

Greg Trawinski, David M. P. Goncalves, Nick DiNuzzo, Alex Rhys, Christopher Vermilya, Jim Fingal, Gavin Craig, Andrew S. Rosenfeld, Ryan Markel, John Hague, William Linn, Greg Cashman, Eric Pidkameny, Alasker, Meghan and Ethan Kaye, Allen Murray, Empty Clip Studios, Mark Freeman, Emerson Emser, James Terry, Kathryn Hemmann, Russell Wiley, Josh Lee, Gavin Graf, douglas riggs, utcv, Corey Losey, Kenny J. Murray, Wesley James Kevin Starr, Philip J Reed, Patrick Tenney, Caleb J. Ross, Victor Romero, Graham Faught, Victor Hunter, Rob Watkins, Stephen Milligan, Eric Tran, Jason Morales, Shawn Clark, Bobby Brankiewicz, Ric Peavyhouse, David Warden, Collin Johnson, Dash Reid, Jason Switzer, Mitchel Labonté, David Portnov, Ashli T., Javy Gwaltney, Royce Rezendes, Andrew Ferguson, Anthony McDonald, Seth Henriksen, Ben Rathert, Patrick Polk, Donald Hopkins, Matthew Millsap, Nate L., Sean Flannigan, Michael Scuderi, vilmibm, Black Lives Matter, John Olson, Malachi Dean Royer, Rusty Collins, Brett Bicksler, Nick Chaimov, Connor Bourn, Nathan Penland, Brayden Egan, Ken Nagasako, Matt Bell, Chris Price, Tamara Henderson, NESJumpman, Ryan Myers, licensetobill, Chris Davis, Nick Henderson, Michael Andrews Dr. Omar Zeid, Samuel DeSarno, Ceth Stifel, Rob H, Heath Bsharah, CK Malone, GigaSeifer, Nick Eliopulos, John Pope, Kyle Hall, Jordan Keith Albaugh, Some Other 1, Steven Vondra II, Bobby Burton, Alvin Yates, Marisa Henriquez, Sam Moseley, Jamie Perez,

Anthony de Jesus, Marq Casarez, Ross Stinemetz, JScott, Eric Wei, Diane Lane, David E., Bryan Mitchell, Kenneth Valentine, Nick Greer, Denham Harry, John Briski, John Boulmetis, Tim Aubel, Armand Tamzarian, B Young, Will Cross, Rob Schmuck, Giovanni Colantonio, Joline, Autumn Beauchesne, Wikipoem.org, Nicholas Limon | @AdventNick, mikecheb, Kelly Ziemski, Tomio Ueda, David Sekowski, Matthew J Riddle, Nick Blesch Clark, Casey Lawler, Mike Davis Jr., Deaven, Mike VK, Justin LaQuay, Jonathan Blue, Zowen, Evgeny Petrov, Brett King, David W. Hill, Ryan F. Feuerhelm, Kristian Watts, Michael Alfieri, Evan Turner, Jonathon Toft-Nielsen, Trevor Starkey, Gregory Lee Englander, TJ Michael, Maxi Organ, J. Asher Henry, D.Dust, James K., Kristen Maloney, Nicole Amato, Patrick King, Geoff McLaughlin, Keegan Chua, Michael Strickland, Dustin Meadows, Aram Kuredjian, thatwhichis, Supercade, Antti Rasanen, Sadozai, Trevor Rodenberger, Philippe Lupien, Bastien Gorissen, Nick Nelson, Andrew Griffin, Matthew Lemay, Hussain Alj, Jay K., John Thomas, Daniel E. Davis (Chainsaw), Keith Travis, Tristan Powell, Joel Bergman, Andy Johnson, Will Salsman, Phil Peterson, Chris Suzuki, Benjamin Hirdler, Joshua Carpenter, Youth in Decline, Zack Johnson, Zac Lovoy, Shannon McCormick, Mark D. Sullivan, and César Augusto Rivera P.

ALSO FROM
BOSS FIGHT BOOKS